Bibliographic information published by the German National Library:

The German National Library lists this publication in the National Bibliography; detailed bibliographic data are available on the Internet at http://dnb.dnb.de .

Imprint:

Copyright © 2009 GRIN Verlag, Open Publishing GmbH
Print and binding: Books on Demand GmbH, Norderstedt Germany
ISBN: 9783640681471

This book at GRIN:

http://www.grin.com/en/e-book/154235/csr-organisational-identification-to-which-extent-do-csr-initiatives

Lucas Rüngeler

CSR & Organisational Identification: To Which Extent Do CSR Initiatives Achieve Organisational Identification?

A Theoretical Review Supported by Empirical Testing in Cooperation with 1492 GmbH and NOKIA

GRIN Publishing

GRIN - Your knowledge has value

Since its foundation in 1998, GRIN has specialized in publishing academic texts by students, college teachers and other academics as e-book and printed book. The website www.grin.com is an ideal platform for presenting term papers, final papers, scientific essays, dissertations and specialist books.

Visit us on the internet:

http://www.grin.com/

http://www.facebook.com/grincom

http://www.twitter.com/grin_com

University of Bayreuth

Cultural Studies Faculty

Philosophy & Economics

Chair of Economics and Business Ethics

Bachelor Thesis

To Earn a Bachelor Degree in Philosophy & Economics

Theme:

CSR & Organisational Identification: To Which Extent Do CSR Initiatives Achieve Organisational Identification?

–

A Theoretical Review Supported by Empirical Testing in Cooperation with a Telecommunications Company

Name	Lucas Rüngeler
Course of Studies	Philosophy & Economics
Term	6

Closing Date   30.03.2009

Table of Contents

Table of Figures

List of Abbreviations

CC	Corporate Citizenship
c.p.	Ceteris paribus
CSP	Corporate Social Performance
CSR	Corporate Social Responsibility
CSR_2	Corporate Social Responsiveness
e.g.	For example
EC	European Commission
EU	European Union
NPS	Net Promoter Score
OCB	Organisational Citizenship Behaviour
OI	Organisational Identification
SIA	Social Identity Approach
SIT	Social Identity Theory
SCT	Self-categorisation Theory

1. Introduction

1.1 Question and Objectives

The identification with organisations plays a prominent role in our lives, since "organizations pervade everyday life"[1]. Usually we are born in a hospital, attend kindergarten, school and other educational institutions until most of us start working for a certain company or organisation in order to make a living for our families and ourselves. Furthermore, many people obtain a membership in various sports clubs, advocacy groups, or parties.[2] Individuals are grateful to such organisations and often make determined efforts for their maintenance, owing to their strong bonds towards these institutions.

Recently, companies have also realised that the identification of their employees is a competitive advantage in many ways. Since organisations "become larger, complex and boundary-less, organisational identification is viewed as a means for providing cohesion and as key ingredient of organisational success"[3]. Based on findings of Bhattacharya and colleagues the individuals' identification with the company results into several positive effects, such as cooperative behaviour, less employee turnover due to higher satisfaction, as well as having strong human capital in terms of knowledge and skills.[4] Accordingly, companies search for drivers that foster positive identification with the organisation.

One driver that has been discovered is seen in corporate social responsibility (CSR) initiatives of companies. The term 'CSR' has received great attention within academic discourses as well as in practice throughout the past decades. CSR is associated with the image that the companies' purpose is more than simply maximising profits. In this respect The Economist notes the following:

> "It would be a challenge to find a recent annual report of any big international company that justifies the firm's existence merely in terms of profit, rather than 'service to the community'."[5]

Another term that is closely related to CSR is that of corporate citizenship (CC). It embraces the notion of business people playing an active role as part of society which is depicted with the help of activities. Whereas CSR is the more academic term referring to the obligation business has to society to respond to social responsibility, CC is rather the managerial term cultivating community-relations such as corporate giving or corporate volunteering. Both concepts shall be the foundation for the understanding of CSR initiatives.

Referring to the ideas of organisational identification (OI) and CSR initiatives introduced above a study by Carmeli and colleagues suggests that CSR initiatives of a company are positively associ-

---

[1] House et al. 1995: 109.
[2] See Van Dick 2004: 1; Böhm 2008: 1.
[3] Epitropaki/Martin 2005: 570. Due to the fact that the thesis is written from the perspective of a firm, organisations are to be understood in the first place as companies.
[4] See Bhattacharya et al. 1995: 46ff.
[5] The Economist 2005.

ated with the employees' identification.[6] Therefore, the paper at hand pursues the following two main objectives:

The *first* objective is to review the correlation between CSR and OI from a theoretical perspective and attempt to provide insights to the underlying question of the present paper: To which extent do CSR initiatives achieve OI? The *second* objective is to bridge theory and practice. In addition to the theoretical review an empirical survey in cooperation with a consultancy and a telecommunications company has been carried out in order to broaden the theoretical view from an empirical perspective.

1.2   Methodology

In order to achieve the main objectives of the thesis, methodologically the elaboration will contain four steps. The *first step* will deal with the concept of CSR, respectively CSR initiatives (chapter 2). It starts with outlining the main streams of the CSR concept in both USA and Europe during the past decades (2.1). Then, theoretical and conceptual basics of CSR initiatives will be presented (2.2). Section 2.2.1 will deal with Carroll's well-known pyramid of CSR, followed by introducing the reader to the more practice-oriented concept of CC (2.2.2). In 2.2.3 elements from both concepts are taken to describe the nature of CSR initiatives in order to establish an underlying understanding for the purpose of the paper. Section 2.3 sketches the usage of such activities to establish lasting relationships with various stakeholders like employees. After explaining basic ideas of stakeholder theory and stakeholder management (2.3.1), the prominent role of employees as being a 'first-class-stakeholder' will be examined. It will be argued that employees play a crucial role in the firms' stakeholder environment and that CSR initiatives may trigger off positive effects on behalf of the firm (2.3.2). One such positive effect is seen in building OI with the firm.

As a consequence, the *second* step will focus on the concept of OI (chapter 3). The purpose is directed to depict a proper understanding of what OI is and why it obtains such useful practical implications for both companies and individuals. Section 3.1 will put forward a theoretical and conceptual framework of OI: Firstly, early scientific approaches will be outlined that describe the nature of identification in the context of organisations (3.1.1). Afterwards the well-known social identity approach (SIA) is discussed, which prevailed as the underlying theoretical framework to explain the concept of OI (3.1.2). Then, in section 3.2 the findings of the SIA are applied to the context of organisations. After defining OI as a specific form of social identification (3.2.1), different conceptualisations in terms of dimensions and foci will be displayed (3.2.2). A model by Dutton and colleagues will illustrate in how far the identity and the image of organisations are associated with OI (3.2.3). Section 3.3 answers the question why OI is useful in many respects.

---

[6] See Carmeli et al. 2007: 973.

Several reasons will be conducted from two different perspectives, one from the perspective of the company (3.3.1), and the other from the individual (3.3.2).

After that, the *third* step bridges step one and two (chapter 4). Building on the theoretical analysis of CSR and OI, the purpose of chapter 4 is to provide insights to the core question of the present thesis: To which extent do CSR initiatives achieve OI? Hence to arrive at suitable results, firstly an understanding of how OI emerges is required. Accordingly, the functional chain will be depicted in section 4.1, which will serve as the underlying model explaining the correlation between CSR and OI. Next, three different approaches will be presented that exist among scientific literature on how (organisational) identification emerges (4.1). In particular these are the processes of affinity (4.2.1), emulation (4.2.2), as well as categorisation and self-enhancement (4.2.3). Drawing upon the three different processes, the entire functional chain will be reconstructed in terms of discussing the link between CSR and OI (4.3). In addition to the theoretical reconstruction, a theoretical review of the current status among scientific literature will be presented as well as a discussion of practice-oriented studies. Ultimately, some deliberations by the author are reflected upon (4.4).

Then, the *fourth* and final step attempts to apply and test the findings of the theoretical analysis to a practice-oriented context (chapter 5). An empirical survey in cooperation with a telecommunications company and a consultancy has been carried out in order to provide additional insights of the theme from another perspective. For reasons of complexity reduction the design of the survey has been simplified to solely two questions that aim to inquire about the employees' degree of being informed about the a telecommunications company's CSR initiatives and about the status of their identification with the telecommunications company community. The results will be presented, discussed and reflected upon.

At the end of the thesis all main aspects of the theoretical review as well as the findings of the empirical testing will be summarised (chapter 6). This will create the basis for a final outlook of the future perspectives in research and practice.

2.   Corporate Social Responsibility

This chapter will introduce the reader to the field of CSR. Building upon stakeholder theory, it will also provide reasons, why employees are to be taken into account as a 'first-class-stakeholder'. Firstly a compact historical overview of CSR will be presented, which will concentrate on CSR in terms of scientific and political developments in both USA and Europe (2.1). Subsequently it will provide a coherent framework that gives meaning and definition to CSR, the frequently cited pyramid of CSR by Carroll will be outlined (2.2.1). Since CC is the more managerial concept and serves best to explain the notion of CSR initiatives, CC will be presented in section 2.2.2. Then, the two concepts of CSR and CC will be demarcated from each other and a preliminary understanding of CSR, respectively to CSR initiatives, will be displayed (2.2.3). Thus, section 2.3 will reveal the prominent role of employees as being a 'first-class-stakeholder'. Accordingly, the elaboration will start with introducing basic ideas of stakeholder theory and stakeholder management (2.3.1). On that score it will be argued that employees play a crucial role in the firms' stakeholder environment and that CSR initiatives can trigger off positive effects on behalf of the firm (2.3.2). Finally, a summarisation of the main aspects will close the chapter (2.4).

2.1 History of Corporate Social Responsibility

The history of the academic field of CSR originated from different branches of research. Essentially different approaches can be identified in the USA and in Europe. The academic discourse in the USA was mainly coined by means of refining definitions and concepts of CSR, whereas in Europe the attention was rather turned toward a pragmatic application.[7]

The launch of the concept of CSR in the 'modern era' of US-literature has been determined by Bowen's book "Social Responsibilities of the Businessman" which was published in 1953.[8] Even though there have been some references to CSR beforehand, his publication is seen as a considerable milestone so that Carroll deems Bowen to be the 'Father of Corporate Social Responsibility'.[9] Bowen argues that companies' actions touch many areas of life which engender the question to what extent business entities are obliged to be taken responsible for the society. He concludes that the social responsibility of businessmen ought to derive from the expectations and values the society upholds and in addition underlines that there are responsibilities which go beyond the economic performance:

> "It [social responsibility (LR)] refers to the obligations of businessmen to pursue those policies, to make those decisions, or to follow those lines of action, which are desirable in terms of the objectives and values of our society."[10]

Accordingly, in the 1960s various authors have proposed several attempts to broaden the first definition set by Bowen. Apart from Frederick (1960), McGuire (1963), and Walton (1967), Davis (1960) has come up with a management oriented view of CSR that focused rather on the social welfare of a society. He postulates that a social responsible business can be justified as far as it

---

[7] See Loew et al. 2004: 18f. Some authors refer to historic roots of CSR. In ancient Greece firms had philanthropic motives distributing money and foot to poor people. Later on in the wake of the 19th century business units changed. More and more multicorporate enterprises occurred that possessed huge influence and power over the market. This emergence of new business entities brought up new questions of responsibilities within society. Then, after the world economic crisis around the 1930s companies were under intensified supervision by the state which conducted into more social activities. For a further review on roots of CSR see Carroll 1999: 268ff.; Carroll/Buchholtz 2006: 31ff.
[8] See Carroll 1979: 497; Carroll 1999: 269. Here Carroll makes the point that earlier articles principally mention Social Responsibility instead of CSR. Carroll utilised both terms synonymously. The paper at hand follows this practise.
[9] See ibid: 268ff. Carroll mentions a few articles that were published prior. For instance he refers to Barnard (1938), Clark (1939) and Kreps (1940).
[10] Bowen 1953: 6.

results into economic gains in the long run.[11] In this context Davis has become well-known for his 'Iron Law of Responsibility' stating that "social responsibilities of businessmen need to be commensurate with their social power"[12]. In addition to this, Davis revisits the understanding of CSR in terms of moving the responsibility from managers towards the influence of whole organisations on society.[13]

In the early 1970s the discussion concerning the significance of CSR on society has turned out to be controversial. Most prominently Friedman's article published in the *New York Times* has contributed to a vivid discourse. Friedman's main message has been that the only social responsibility of business is to maximize profits within the legal frame.[14] Also, at the same time CSR definitions have proliferated and have become more specific due to works by various authors.[15] In 1979 Carroll released a renowned article on the conception of a three-dimensional model of corporate social performance (CSP) and picks up certain notions of prior CSR definitions.[16] The categorisation of the four different social responsibilities was developed further by Watrick/Cochran. They presented an extended revision of the three dimensional integration of responsibility, responsiveness and social issues by Carroll. It has been argued that Carroll's CSR definition merely covered the ethical component. In their view social responsibility should be viewed as *principals*, social responsiveness as a *process* and social issues management as *policies*.[17] A next step in the academic discourse has been done by Wood. She expands the CSP approach and outlines a CSP model that captures CSR concerns. Nevertheless she sharply distinguishes between drawing up categorisations and principles.[18]

The emergence of the CSR concept in Europe has occurred much later.[19] In particular it has been politics, more precisely the European Union (EU), which put emphasis on the social responsibility of companies.[20] The starting point has been the so called *Lisbon Strategy*[21] which was set out by the European Council in March 2000. Its aim has been "to become the most competitive and

---

[11] See Davis 1960: 70f. Carroll remarks that Davis' view is interesting because it became commonly accepted later in the 1970s and 1980s. See Carroll 1999: 271.
[12] Davis 1960: 71.
[13] See Davis 1967: 46. "Social responsibility moves one large step further by emphasizing institutional actions and their effect on the whole social system. Social responsibility, therefore, broadens a person's view to the total social system" (Davis 1967: 46).
[14] See Friedman 1970: 32f. Carroll points out that Friedman's statements were understood in different ways. He interprets Friedman in a way that only the philanthropic responsibility is rejected. See Carroll 1991: 43.
[15] See Carroll 1999: 291 and the cited literature.
[16] "The social responsibility of business encompasses the economic, legal, ethical and discretionary expectations that society has of organisations at a given point of time" (Carroll 1979: 500). Carroll's pyramid of CSR will be explained in detail later on. See section 2.2.1.
[17] See Wartick/Cochran 1985: 758ff.; Carroll 1999: 287.
[18] See Wood 1991: 695. "A principle expresses something fundamental that people believe is true, or it is a basic value that motivates people to act" (Wood 1991: 695).
[19] One exception is Great Britain. See Loew et al. 2004: 24.
[20] See for the following Ibid: 24ff.
[21] Also known as Lisbon Agenda or Lisbon Process.

dynamic knowledge-based economy in the world, capable of sustainable economic growth with more and better jobs and greater social cohesion"[22]. One year later the European Commission (EC) released both, the EU strategy[23] for a sustainable development and a Green Paper with the mission statement "Promoting a European Framework for Corporate Social Responsibility".[24] Here, the first time a definition of CSR is displayed by a political European institution:[25]

> "[...] a concept whereby companies integrate social and environmental concerns in their business operations and in their interaction with their stakeholders on a voluntary basis."[26]

Against the background of the Green Paper more activities have been undertaken in support of CSR. In 2004 the so called 'European Multistakeholder Forum on CSR' was established to foster the dialogue between experts, stakeholders[27] and companies.[28] Then, in 2006 the EC called for an 'Alliance on Corporate Social Responsibility' bringing together mainly industry actors and the Commission.[29]

On the whole one can summarize a stronger focus on CSR issues at the beginning of the 21st century. In contrast to the academic discourse on CSR in the USA, the main attention in Europe has been placed on political guidance.

2.2   Theoretical and Conceptual Framework of CSR Initiatives

2.2.1   Corporate Social Responsibility

Besides the understanding of CSR, other closely related concepts have evolved from scientific debate, which include *corporate social responsiveness*[30](CSR_2) and *corporate social performance*[31],[32] Other

---

[22] European Council 2000: http://www.consilium.europa.eu/ueDocs/cms_Data/docs/pressData/en/ec/00100-r1.en0.htm.

[23] See European Commission 2001b: http://eur-lex.europa.eu/LexUriServ/LexUriServ.do?uri=COM:2002:0347: FIN:DE: PDF.

[24] See European Commission 2001a: http://eur-lex.europa.eu/LexUriServ/site/en/com/2001/_0366en01.pdf.

[25] See Loew et al. 2004: 26.

[26] European Commission 2001a: 7.

[27] See section 2.3.1 for further details on stakeholders and stakeholder theory.

[28] See EMS Forum 2004: http://circa.europa.eu/irc/empl/csr_eu_multi_stakeholder_forum/info /data /en /CSR %20Forum%20final%20report.pdf.

[29] See European Commission 2006: 3. http://eur-lex.europa.eu/LexUriServ/LexUriServ.do?uri=COM:2006:0136 :FIN: EN:PDF. This paper provoked anger from civil society organisations as well as trade unions. They criticise that NGOs are largely excluded from the CSR alliance because it only brings together the Commission and enterprises. See http://www.euractiv.com/en/socialeurope/csr-corporate-social-responsibility/article-153515.

[30] Corporate Social Responsiveness (CSR_2) is considered as the action-oriented variant of CSR. According to Frederick CSR_2 is defined as follows: "Corporate social responsiveness refers to the capacity of a corporation to respond to social pressures. The literal act of responding, or of achieving a generally responsive posture, to society is the focus" (Frederick 1978: 6). See also further authors that contributed to ideas of CSR_2: Ackerman/Bauer 1976: 6; Epstein 1987: 104.

[31] Building on ideas of CSR, Carroll developed first a model of CSP. It includes three aspects that address major concerns of academics and managers, in particular CSR, social issues the organisation must address and the mode of social responsiveness. See Carroll 1979: 497ff. A major reformulation of the CSP model has been put forward by Wood. She defines CSP as the "business organization's configuration of principles of social responsibility, processes of social responsiveness, and policies, programs, and observable outcomes as they relate to the firm's societal relationships" (Wood 1991: 693). Other extensions of the CSP model have been presented by Wartick/Cochran 1985: 765-766 and Swanson 1995: 43-64 as well as Swanson 1999: 506-521.

[32] See Carroll/Buchholtz 2006: 29.

affiliated concepts can also be seen in *corporate philanthropy*[33] and *corporate governance*[34]. Since a detailed presentation of each concept would go beyond the scope of the thesis at hand, and CSR as well as CC serve best for the purposes of how CSR initiatives are supposed to be understood, the following will focus merely on CSR and CC.

One of the most well-known concepts of CSR was introduced by Carroll. According to his concept a firm is obliged to respond to social responsibility in four different components.

> "For a definition of social responsibility to fully address the entire range of obligations business has to society, it must embody the economic, legal, ethical and discretionary categories of business performance."[35]

Within his article Carroll puts emphasis on the fact that these four categories are not mutually excluded from each other, nor that they are supposed to sketch a continuum with economic motives on the one hand and social concerns on the other.[36] It is rather intended to portray the total CSR of a company which enables us to classify certain motives or actions according to the different responsibilities that constitute the whole. Figure 1 visualizes Carroll's pyramid of CSR:[37]

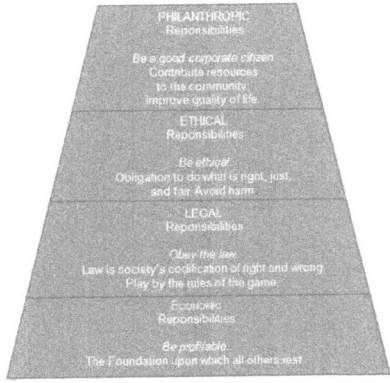

Figure 1: The Pyramid of Corporate Social Responsibility.
Source: Carroll 1991: 42.

The *economic responsibility* is located at the basis of the pyramid. Business organisations were established to be the basic unit within society. As such a firms' duty is to produce goods and services

---

[33] According to Carroll/Buchholtz Corporate Philanthropy is considered as "the voluntary giving of financial resources by business" (Ibid: 480). Therefore, as firms give resources on a voluntarily basis, the concept of corporate philanthropy has a lot in common with the understanding of corporate citizenship (see 2.2.2). Amongst others a frequently noted article has been put forward by Porter/Kramer on the benefits of strategic corporate philanthropy: "True strategic giving [...] addresses important social and economic goals simultaneously, targeting areas of competitive context where the company and society both benefit because the firm brings unique assets and expertise" (Porter/Kramer 2002: 60).
[34] "Corporate Governance deals with the agency problem: the separation of management and finance. The fundamental question of corporate governance is how to assure financiers that they get a return on their financial investment" (Shleifer/Vishney 1997: 773).
[35] Carroll 1979: 499.
[36] See ibid: 499.
[37] See for the review on the distinct responsibilities Carroll 1979: 499f.; Carroll 1991: 40ff.; Carroll 2000: 26f.; Promberger/Spiess 2006: 8ff.

to provide for the consumers' needs and to contribute to the societies' wealth. The motive for profit is the driving force for entrepreneurship. Therefore, all other business responsibilities rely on the economic responsibility of the firm due to the fact that the others rest upon this foundation. Acknowledging this, a firm is required to operate under *legal responsibilities*. Among the economic system certain ground rules have been laid down under which business is expected to play its economic role. Business units are expected to comply with the laws and regulations society has installed. As a consequence the firm, as a law-abiding player, is forced to respect and not to infringe this 'social contract' between business and society. Since the legal responsibilities mirror 'codified ethics', fundamental principals of fair operations are depicted within this framework of law. The *ethical responsibilities* comprise these activities and practices as well. On the contrary they are not codified into law and represent the norms and values of a society. Insofar ethical responsibilities indicate what extent societal members would regard as fair and just. Considering that such values and norms may mirror higher standards of ethical performance than currently required by law, it is inevitable to meet the expectations society has of business. Therefore, "ethical responsibilities in this sense are often ill-defined or continually under public debate as to their legitimacy, and thus are frequently difficult for business to deal with"[38]. In this respect it is also set forth that ethical and legal responsibilities always deal with a dynamic interplay. That is, legal responsibilities are to be developed further to ethical standards, and therefore businessmen are constantly confronted with growing expectations to conduct according to higher ethical responsibilities. The last category is labelled as discretionary responsibilities. Later Carroll renamed this term to *philanthropic responsibilities* due to the fact that being philanthropic is of a more voluntarily notion than being discretionary consistent with the image of a good corporate citizen.[39] Thus, acknowledging voluntariness as the underlying foundation for philanthropy, it covers all the actions of a company that go beyond what is explicitly expected from the society. Hence, contribution to any humanitarian programs – the arts, education, or the community – are left to individual judgement and choice because a firm is not regarded as unethical if they do not comply with the favoured level. In that sense, according to the pyramid displayed in Figure 1, Carroll makes use of a metaphor maintaining that the philanthropic responsibilities are like "icing on the cake"[40]. In summarization Carroll postulates the following how to pursue his CSR concept:

> "The CSR firm should strive to make a profit, obey the law, be ethical, and be a good corporate citizen."[41]

---

[38] Carroll 1991: 41. For instance, business has to deal with environmental, civil rights, or consumer movements which are able to exert pressure on the fulfilment of ethical responsibilities.
[39] See section 2.2.2 for further details on CC.
[40] Carroll 1991: 42.
[41] Ibid: 43.

The view of being a good corporate citizen is rather used in a practice-oriented managerial context and serves as an inclusive reference to issues linked to social responsibility.[42] From this practice-oriented perspective the idea of the so called *triple bottom line* has gathered wide acceptance among practitioners, since it provides guidance in terms of operationalisation. It refers to the expanded notion that the criteria for the creation of value are economic, ecological and social.[43] Since CSR initiatives address activities exerted in the field with a managerial component, the concept of CC is outlined in the subsequent section.

2.2.2 Corporate Citizenship

According to Carroll/Buchholtz the understanding of CSR has been embraced to the broader term of CC. Hereby, CC illustrates a conception of business actors that play an active role as part of society. The concept of the corporate citizen reflects the core idea of a civil society in which all participants themselves carry responsibility for the well-being of the community.[44] Although a widely accepted definition of CC is not established yet, CC has been subject of various interpretations in both USA and Europe.[45] Among scientific literature in the USA, Carroll articulates that CC can be conceived from a *broad view* and a *narrow view*.[46]

The *broad view* suggests that CC encompasses all that is implied in the concepts of CSR, CSR_2 and CSP. For instance, a broad conception has been put forward by Fombrun, who argues that CC is composed of a three-part view: (1) CC is the reflection of shared ethical and moral principles, (2) a vehicle to integrate individuals into the communities in which they work, and (3) a form of enlightened self-interest, which balances all stakeholders' demands and enriches a firm's long-term value.[47] Especially, the notion of the firms' self-interest is according to the broad view a typical characteristic. CC explicitly focuses on the achievement of win-win-situations, meaning that CC is also part of the overall business strategy. That is why Graves and colleagues define CC as "serving a variety of stakeholders well"[48] which embraces the idea of ethical business behaviour and

---

[42] See Carroll/Buchholtz 2006: 38f. See also footnote 50 for a criticism by Crane/Matten.
[43] "[...] the TBL [Triple Bottom Line, (LR)] agenda focuses corporations not just on the economic value that they add, but also on the environmental and social value that they add – and destroy" (Elkington 2001: 3). See also Loew et al. 2004: 66f.
[44] See Bowie 1991: 58ff.; Loew et al. 2004: 50; Beckmann/Pies 2008: 110f. A starting point for the introduction of corporate citizenship is seen in the programme 'Habit for Humanity' initiated by the former US-President Jimmy Carter. The programme dealt with the discussion about the relationship between companies and their role inside society. Later on in the 1990s the term 'corporate citizenship' emerged as a new form of addressing the social role of companies among scientific literature. See Carroll 1999: 290; Crane/Matten 2007: 70. Carroll also finds first roots of CC among literature in the 1960s. See Carroll 1999: 271f.
[45] See Crane/Matten 2007: 70f.
[46] See Carroll 1999: 290; Carroll/Buchholtz 2006: 54. Crane/Matten distinguish among literature three different perspectives: A limited view of CC that equates CC with corporate philanthropy, an equivalent view of CC which equates CC with CSR and an extended view of CC which acknowledges the extended political role of the corporation in society. See Crane/Matten 2007: 71ff.; Garriga/Melé 2004: 56f.
[47] See Fombrun 1997: 27ff.
[48] Graves et al. 2001: 17.

the balancing of the needs of stakeholders.[49] After all, in a recap of the four categories of CSR, Carroll argues in his article "The Four Faces of Corporate Citizenship" that companies are expected to fulfil the four responsibilities of being economic, legal, ethical, and philanthropic like private citizens.[50]

Concerning the *narrow view*, CC is understood in terms of corporate community relations suggesting that the firm behaves as a 'good citizen'.[51] This view, which is predominantly held in Europe, embraces the functions through which a firm intentionally collaborates with non-profit organisations, citizen groups, and other stakeholders at the community level.[52] Acknowledging this view of Anglo-American discussion, various authors from Germany have adopted this understanding.[53] Westebbe/Logan indicate that only those activities are classed among CC, which go beyond primary business activities.[54] As such according to Mutz/Korfmacher CC includes corporate giving, corporate foundations, and corporate volunteering.[55]

Corporate giving comprises contributing money towards a fund or charitable purposes as well as sponsoring, whereas *corporate foundations* stand for the establishment of charitable foundations.[56] *Corporate volunteering* is considered as company measures which grant leave to employees from regular work in order to let them participate in welfare work or in similar activities.[57]

---

[49] See further details on stakeholder theory in section 2.3.1.

[50] See Carroll 1998: 1ff. Crane/Matten harshly criticise Carroll's conceptualisation of CC. From their point of view Carroll's understanding of CC "consists in a somewhat updated label for CSR (or sometimes stakeholder management), without attempting to define any new role or responsibilities for the corporation" (Crane/Matten 2007: 73). Before Carroll published his article referring to CC in 1998, he identified being a good corporate citizen with his fourth level of CSR, in particular the philanthropic responsibility. See also section 2.2.1.

[51] See Carroll/Buchholtz 2006: 54.

[52] See Ibid; Schwalbach/Schwerk 2008: 78f.

[53] See Loew et al. 2004: 52f. Loew and colleagues mention three different streams that discuss CC from different perspectives within the German debate: (1) CC in terms of economic and business ethics, (2) CC carried out by business that goes beyond primary business activities, and (3) CC in terms of discussing sustainability. See Loew et al. 2004: 53f. A frequently cited definition for sustainability has been put forward by the so called Brundtland Commission: "Sustainable development is development that meets the needs of the present without comprising the ability of future generations to meet their own needs" (Brundtland 1987: 43).

[54] See Westebbe/Logan 1995: 13. "Corporate Citizenship ist das gesamte koordinierte, einer einheitlichen Strategie folgende und über die eigentliche Geschäftätigkeit hinausgehende Engagement des Unternehmens zur Lösung gesellschaftlicher Probleme" (Westebbe/Logan 1995: 13, German definition). In contrast to Westebbe/Logan, who exclude CC from core business activities, the World Economic Forum puts forward a different view: "Corporate Citizenship is about the contribution a company makes to society through its core business activities, its social investment and philanthropy programmes, and its engagement in public policy" (World Economic Forum 2003: 17). See also Beckmann 2007: 6.

[55] See Mutz/Korfmacher 2003: 51f.; Loew et al. 2004: 53. Furthermore, Dresewski mentions nine instruments of a so called 'Corporate Citizenship-Mix': Corporate Giving, Corporate Foundations, Corporate Volunteering, Social Sponsoring, Cause Related Marketing, Social Commissioning, Community Joint Venture, Social Lobbying and Venture Philanthropy. See Dresewski 2004: 21f. and also Habisch 2003: 97ff.

[56] See Maaß/Clemens 2002: 11ff.; Loew et al. 2004: 53. According to some authors corporate giving and corporate foundations encompass the same and are therefore an equation is made with the two terms. See Bruhn 1998: 20.

[57] See Schöffmann 2001: 14; Maaß/Clemens 2002: 13f.; Herzig 2005: 5. Various companies have implemented corporate volunteering into their overall CSR strategy. Among others, the Deutsche Bank AG can be mentioned as an example. See Frankfurter Allgemeine Zeitung 2008: B2.

2.2.3 CSR and CC as Basis for the Understanding of CSR Initiatives

To agree upon the relation between CSR and CC a demarcation of the two concepts has been put forward by various authors. According to Beckmann three different suggestions exist amid the scientific literature: Firstly, CC is understood as the superior concept whereas CSR only plays a partial aspect.[58] Secondly, some advocate that CSR is the superior concept, which embraces the firm's activities as a good corporate citizen.[59] And thirdly, this view equates the concepts of CSR and CC, which are solely seen as alternative explanations for the description of the same phenomenon.[60]

In order to arrive at an understanding of *CSR initiatives*, the paper at hand combines the notions of CSR and CC to flow into an explanation. Whereas CSR is the more academic term referring to the obligation business has to society to respond to social responsibility, CC is rather the managerial term cultivating community-relations. Accordingly, the notion of CSR and CC shall be subsumed to CSR initiatives in a rather broad sense defining CSR initiatives on the part of the firm as "actions that appear to further some social good, beyond the interests of the firm and that what is required by law"[61]. These actions include concrete activities described in terms of the narrow CC view such as corporate giving, corporate foundations, and corporate volunteering in order to foster a socially-based purpose or a stakeholder group.[62] Therefore, CSR initiatives are intimately tied to the firms' relationship with its stakeholders, indicating that the social obligations of business have specific nonmarket environment beneficiaries whose demands and expectations must be met by the firms' performance.[63] The ethical behaviour of firms will enable them to achieve competitive advantages, because they develop lasting relationships with stakeholders.[64] As CSR initiatives also reveal the values of a company, they can also be part of the value proposition of a stakeholder with which he can identify.[65]

In this context it shall be noted that it is not enough just to enact CSR initiatives. At the same time companies must have in focus on the accuracy of their communication so that stakeholders become aware in how far the firm is pursuing CSR. Companies have several instruments available in order to inform their workforce about their CSR such as regular CSR reports, newsletters, or

---

[58] See Loew et al. 2004: 54 and the cited literature.

[59] See Ibid; Wood/Logsdon: 84ff.

[60] See Beckmann 2007: 6f. Matten and colleagues claim that the concepts of CSR and CC have been used synonymously. They refer to Carroll's article "The Four Faces of Corporate Citizenship", in which he defines CC the same way as he defined CSR. See Matten et al. 2003: 112f.

[61] McWilliams/Siegel 2001: 117. Tetrault Sirsly/Lammertz note that McWilliams/Siegel have absorbed their definition of CSR initiatives from Burke/Logsdon. See Tetrault Sirsly/Lammertz 2008: 348; Burke/Logsdon 1996: 495.

[62] See McWilliams/Siegel 2001: 117; Carroll/Buchholtz 2006: 55; Godfrey/Hatch: 2007: 88; Carmeli et al. 2007: 976.

[63] See Waddock et al. 2002: 145f.

[64] See Jones 1995: 404ff.; McWilliams/Siegel 2001: 118.

[65] See Bhattacharya et al. 2008: 37.

seminars. Also, a typical CC-activity like corporate volunteering is an excellent tool not just to involve stakeholders and make them aware of the firms' CSR.[66]

Since CSR initiatives improve the connection to companies' stakeholders, the following section will deal with basic ideas of stakeholder theory and stakeholder management and will reveal the eminent role employees play among various stakeholders.

2.3   The Usage of CSR Initiatives To Establish Lasting Stakeholder-Group Relationships With Employees

2.3.1   Basic Ideas of Stakeholder Theory & Stakeholder Management

In his article "The Pyramid of Corporate Social Responsibility" Carroll provides a segue from CSR to stakeholder theory, since the stakeholder concept personalises social or societal responsibilities by sketching the individuals and specific groups the firm ought to take into account in its CSR orientation. Therefore, "names and faces"[67] are put on stakeholders, which are most important to the firm and to which it must be responsive so that it turns attention beyond direct profit maximisation.[68] While CSR aims to determine what responsibilities business ought to fulfil, the stakeholder concept addresses the issues of whom the firm should be accountable to. In this sense both concepts are closely inter-related, while CSR can be interpreted as a branch of stakeholder theory.[69]

Originally stakeholder theory is a concept that is derived from strategic management. Strategic management is a systematic way to solve the firms' problems. According to Ansoff the objectives of strategic management are the future continuity, survival and profitability of the firm.[70] For the first time the usage of the term stakeholder grew out of the pioneering work of the Stanford Research Institute[71] in 1963, which was developed in the planning department of Lockheed.[72] Stakeholders are put into the description as "those groups without whose support the organization would cease to exist"[73], whereas each stakeholder has one or more of various kinds of stakes in a

---

[66] See Breidenbach et al. 2008: 23f. The aspect to inform employees about the firms' CSR initiatives will especially become relevant in chapter 5 according to the empirical survey.

[67] Carroll 1991: 43.

[68] See Carroll 1991: 43; Ibid. 1999: 290. "There is a natural fit between the idea of corporate social responsibility and an organization's stakeholders" (Carroll 1991: 43).

[69] See Wentges 2002: 95f.; Foster/Jonker 2005: 51ff.; Jamali 2008: 228.

[70] See Ansoff 1979: 1. Etymologically, the word 'strategy' comes from the context of ancient Greek warfare, where it refers to the art of leading an army. At the beginning of the 19th century, the terminus was rediscovered by the Prussian Major-General and intellectual Carl von Clausewitz. In his famous book "About War" (German: "Vom Kriege") he defined strategy as the general set of guidelines, in contrast to tactic, which is just a situational reaction to external stimuli.

[71] Today it is rather known as the SRI International. See http://www.sri.com.

[72] It is not by chance that the term stakeholder is relatively similar to the term of stockholder. The purpose has been to express that there are other groups, which have a stake in the firm compared to the stockholders. See Göbel 2006: 113.

[73] Freeman 1984: 31. See also Freeman/McVea 2001: 190f. and Brink 2002: 66f. "[...] managers needed to understand the concerns of shareholders, employees, customers, suppliers, lenders and society, in order to develop objectives that stakeholders would support. This support was necessary for long term success. Therefore, management should actively explore its relationships with all stakeholders in order to develop business strategies" (Freeman/McVea 2001: 190).

business.[74] The most popular definition of stakeholder has been developed by Freeman in his noted work "Strategic Management: A Stakeholder Approach" in which he outlines a new approach to strategic management tasks. Freeman defines the term stakeholder as follows:

> "A stakeholder in an organization is (by definition) any group or individual who can affect or is affected by the achievement of the organization's objectives."[75]

This definition is widely acknowledged because of its "landmark"[76] position in stakeholder theory.[77] As a matter of fact stakeholder theory has been subject to be presented in a number of ways, since it is a state of the art concept within strategic management literature. Donaldson/Preston have put forward a frequently cited categorisation of stakeholder approaches that articulates three views of the stakeholder model of the firm, which are in particular a *descriptive*, an *instrumental* and a *normative* view.[78]

The *descriptive* view provides information about how reality is. Accordingly, stakeholder theory is used in a descriptive way to mirror the internal and external reality of the firms' environment and describes the actual practice in what way a company deals with its stakeholders.[79] According to the *instrumental* view it is useful to establish connections between practical implications of the stakeholder theory and the resulting achievement of traditional corporate performance goals such

---

[74] See Carroll/Buchholtz 2006: 67. Roots of stakeholder theory are also to find further in the past according to Berle/Means (1932). A further development can also be identified in the context of the stimulus-contribution theory. Important advocates are Barnard (1938), March/Simon (1958) and Cyert/March (1963) who especially focus on the the behavioural theory of the firm. See also for an overview Wentges 2002: 88ff. and Brink 2002: 67.

[75] Freeman 1984: 46. Furthermore, often a less wide definition is mentioned that has been developed by Freeman/Reed. According to them a stakeholder is "(a)ny identifiable group or individual on which the organization is dependent for its continued survival" (Freeman/Reed 1983: 91).

[76] Wood 1991: 704.

[77] Today's companies are embedded in a network of mutual dependence with numerous stakeholders. To arrive at this view, the stakeholder concept parallels the evolution of a business enterprise. The starting point for Freeman's considerations is formerly described by the *production view of the firm*. The production view sees the company as family-owned business, which brings products to the market. Efficiency and effectiveness of this process were the key factors to success. Over time large firms have emerged as being economically more successful due to scale effects in production and the usage of better production techniques, as e.g. assembly lines. As a consequence of the increasing need for capital banks, stockholders and other financing institutions began to dominate the company. This development resulted in the evolution that can be titled as the *managerial view of the firm*. The management had to pay attention to more groups of people, who have a stake in the firm, than they had before. In the production view only the market, i.e. customers, and suppliers, mattered to the management, whereas they now additionally have to deal with the interests of the company's owners and their workers. See Freeman 1984: 4 and also Carroll/Buchholtz 2006: 68ff. Finally, as major internal and external changes were to occur in business and firms had to undergo its multilateral relationships, Freeman's suggestion to meet this new environment, is to "redraw the picture of the firm" (Freeman 1984: 24) in terms of the *stakeholder view of the firm*. In this view the management must perceive its stakeholders not merely in the way that they have some stake in the firm, but also the stakeholders have a stake in the firm as well. So the idea is to develop individual strategies for each group of stakeholders. Those strategies are thought to be more efficient in influencing the stakeholders' decision whether to provide the company with their resources or not in a favourable way, since they address the various interests of stakeholders individually. See Freeman 1984: 25; Post et al. 2002: 51ff.

[78] See Donaldson/Preston 1995: 66ff. See also Jones/Wicks 1999: 212 who discuss the significance of Donaldson and Prestons's scheme. Another way to address different stakeholders has been advanced by Goodpaster, who distinguishes among the strategic approach, the multifiduciary approach, and the stakeholder synthesis approach. See Goodpaster 1991: 53ff.

[79] See Donaldson/Preston 1995: 70. See also for an overview of works that argue in favour of the descriptive view Wentges 2002: 94.

as profitability, stability and growth. Mostly on the basis of empirical studies, advocates of the instrumental view try to prove that a firm carrying trough stakeholder management c.p. will attain better results relative to others.[80] From the *normative* point of view stakeholders are identified by their interest in the firm, regardless of whether the firm has a corresponding interest in them. Stakeholders, thus, have an intrinsic value, which qualifies them for being cared about by the management of the firm, so that they are never regarded merely as a means to an end. Consequently, the normative perspective is frequently considered as the moral or ethical view due to the fact that it concentrates on how stakeholders *should* be treated.[81] In summarisation of the three different views Donaldson/Preston conclude that stakeholder theory is *managerial* in the sense that it does not simply describe but also advises attitudes, structures and practices which frame stakeholder management.[82]

With respect to the three different views, a differentiation can be made according to two concepts of stakeholder management: the *strategic* stakeholder management and the *intrinsic* stakeholder management. The descriptive and the instrumental views are subsumed into the strategic approach, which pursues a stakeholder management by means of generating positive effects contributing to the overall firms' performance. On the contrary the normative view is linked to the intrinsic stakeholder management, which can be understood as a "normative (moral) commitment to treating stakeholders in a positive way"[83], which in turn also increases positive effects of the corporate performance.[84]

2.3.2   Identification of Employees as First-Class-Stakeholder-Group

Stakeholder management has become important, since managers have discovered that many stakeholders ought to be satisfied in order to meet the firms' objectives.[85] As each stakeholder pursues different interests which mutually influence each other, the challenging task is therefore, to balance in between the area of conflict of diverse interests. However, basically not all stakes in the firm are legitimate a priori.[86] Insofar it must be clarified in how far the firms' management is

---

[80] "If you want to achieve (avoid) results X, Y or Z, then adopt (don't adopt) principles and practices A, B, or C" (Donaldson/Preston 1995: 72). The major problem with empirical studies, which seek to show such a correlation, is that they can hardly deliver representative data. There are numerous factors that influence a companies' performance, which cannot be kept constant in order to isolate the influence of the utilisation of stakeholder principles. Donaldson/Preston therefore conclude that there hasn't been a study yet, which represents solid evidence for the superiority of stakeholder management. See Donaldson/Preston 1995: 71ff. and 77; Donaldson 1999: 238. On the contrary Harrison/John put emphasis on the positive significance for companies: "We should do it because it is the right thing to do" (Harrison/John 1996: 48). See also Talaulicar 2006: 60f. for further details and an overview on arguments in favour of the instrumental view.

[81] See Wentges 2002: 95; Carroll/Buchholtz 2006: 74.

[82] See Donaldson/Preston 1995: 67; Carroll/Buchholtz 2006: 75.

[83] Berman et al. 1999: 488.

[84] See Ibid: 493f.; Brink 2002: 71f.

[85] See Carroll/Buchholtz 2006: 75.

[86] See for further details and an overview on the different stakes stakeholder hold Janisch 1993: 145ff.; Brink 2000: 199ff.

supposed to take into account the stakes of the various stakeholders. Consequently, to manage stakeholders effectively, each firm has to answer the question "who are our stakeholders?"[87].

Among literature a few approaches have been put forward to classify stakeholders according to their significance for the firm.[88] Clarkson distinguishes between *primary* and *secondary* stakeholders, whereas the primary stakeholder group is the one without whose continuing participation the firm cannot survive as a going concern. Accordingly, profitable companies can be differentiated from others that in the past have created wealth and value for all its primary stakeholder groups. In contrast, the secondary stakeholder group is not essential for the firms' survival.[89]

Encompassing the employees as focus against the background of the paper at hand, it is prevalently accepted that employees are one of the most important stakeholders a firm has. Regardless whether one acknowledges Clarkson's categorisation of stakeholder groups, which puts employees in the group of primary stakeholders, or one screens other noted approaches of stakeholder categorisations, effectively in all respects *employees* are considered "to take on a peculiar role among stakeholders as they are closely integrated to the firm"[90,91].

From the *firms' perspective*, employees have significant influence on the firm, since they belong to one of the most important 'resources' a company obtains in terms of knowledge and skills. In particular, in an information- and knowledge-based strategy era in which continuing shortage of highly skilled and talented workers is expected, employees are the basis of potential competitive advantage.[92] Furthermore, they represent the company towards other stakeholders, such as customers, the local community and so forth, and besides act in the name of the firm towards them.[93] On the contrary, from the *employees' perspective* they are greatly affected by the success or failure of the company, since they are dependent on income.

---

[87] Vos 2003: 142. See also Carroll/Buchholtz 2006: 76; Talaulicar 2006: 63. With reference to the definition posited by Freeman presented above, almost every entity in the business environment could be a potential stakeholder. So the question after the "principle of who or what really count" (Freeman 1994: 411) is unanswered.

[88] A frequently cited typology of stakeholder attributes has been put forward by Mitchell and colleagues. The three attributes of legitimacy, power, and urgency help to discover how stakeholders can be assessed. Their typology contributed to support the instrumental view of stakeholder theory. See Mitchell et al. 1997: 872ff.; Carroll/Buchholtz 2006: 71ff.

[89] See Clarkson 1995: 105ff. Other authors have put forward a relatively similar categorisation between primary and secondary stakeholders. Among others these are Harrison/John 1996: 47f.; Donaldson/Dunfee 1999: 167; Wheeler/Sillanpää 1997: 167.

[90] Crane/Matten 2007: 265.

[91] Furthermore deep roots of stakeholder theory refer to employees as an important stakeholder group. See Berle/Means 1932: 355; Dodd 1932: 38; Cyert/March 1967: 27.

[92] See Waddock et al. 2002: 135.

[93] See Crane/Matten 2007: 265; Greenwood 2008: 3.

Referring to concepts of institutional economics, some authors highlight the high risk sensibility of employees in terms of their specific investment into their employer.[94] Moreover, employees make a substantial investment in their work, given they make geographical moves, obtain strong relationships within the firm, or invest into further training in order to improve their career opportunities. Accordingly, it is widely accepted that employees obtain a definite stake in the firm.[95] With respect to the managers' tasks of stakeholder management, relationships to employees as some kind of *first-class-stakeholder-group* are essential for the well-being of the firm according to both, strategic and intrinsic stakeholder management. It is strategic, as managing such relationships can result not only in a continued participation in the companies' concerns, it can also evoke socially complex resources that enable the firm to gain a competitive advantage compared to others.[96] In addition, some authors claim that building strong relationships with employees contributes in the sense of driving the financial performance.[97] In terms of intrinsic stakeholder management, since employees are in many ways affected by the companies' success and also invest personally, they obtain a moral claim in the firm so that companies are more or less obliged to regard the employees' stakes.[98] Hence, referring to both sorts of stakeholder management, a company has in either way a deep interest to build strong bonds with their employees, since they belong to one of the most substantial primary stakeholder.

As outlined in section 2.2.3, CSR initiatives further a socially based purpose or stakeholder groups, in particular they stress the importance of actions towards employees in various ways. A study by Carmeli and colleagues suggests that CSR initiatives of a company are positively associated with the employees' identification.[99] Since the underlying question of this paper is to which extent CSR initiatives achieve identification in terms of organisations, the next chapter will focus on the elaboration on OI.

2.4   Intermediate Result

The purpose of this chapter has been to introduce the reader to the field of CSR, to reveal the nature of CSR initiatives and to highlight why employees play a special role among stakeholders. Section 2.1 gave an overview of the *history* the concept of CSR has undergone in both, USA and Europe. While in the USA primarily CSR has been subject to academic discourse in order to dis-

---

[94] See Blair 2003: 57; Soppe 2008: 218; Brink 2009: 6. "The downside risk of the employee is considered the most severe of all stakeholders. Because of the long term and long term fixed contracts, employees have a vulnerable bargaining position in the sticky labour market. Most important is the fact that employees cannot easily diversify their labour contracts. This makes the individual employee the most vulnerable party in this stockholder's approach of the market economy" (Soppe 2008: 218). The notion of the importance of risk is also stressed by Clarkson. In this sense a stake is something that can be lost. See Clarkson 1995: 112.
[95] See Crane/Matten 2007: 265; Greenwood 2008: 3.
[96] See Burke/Logsdon 1995: 495ff.; Hillman/Keim 2001: 127; Tetrault Sirsly/Lamertz 2008: 350ff.
[97] See Atkinson et al. 1997: 30ff.
[98] See Kaler 2002: 91ff.
[99] See Carmeli et al. 2007: 976.

cuss upon concepts and definitions, the attention to CSR in Europe has been concentrated rather by political institutions. Then, section 2.2 served to develop an understanding of what *CSR initiatives* are. Firstly, Carroll's widely accepted pyramid of CSR has been presented, suggesting that a firm is obliged to respond to *social responsibility* according to four different components. This obligation embodies an *economic, legal, ethical, and discretionary (philanthropic) responsibility* (2.2.1). Furthermore, the practice-oriented approach of the so called triple bottom line has been noted, which refers to economic, ecological and social criteria for the creation of value. Secondly, since CSR initiatives are associated with concrete activities within society, the concept of CC has been introduced (2.2.2). The core idea of CC is that business actors as part of civil society play an active role for the well-being of the community. Referring to scientific discourse in the USA, CC has been presented from a *broad* and a *narrow view*. The broad view of CC encompasses all that is implied in the closely related concepts such as CSR, CSR_2 or CSP. From this point of view, CC appears to achieve win-win-situations in order to serve a variety of stakeholders well. On the contrary the narrow view focuses on actions that sustain the corporate community relations a company upholds. This understanding of CC has mainly gained recognition by authors from Europe, respectively from Germany. Such business activities include corporate giving, corporate foundations, and corporate volunteering. After proposing three different suggestions in what way CSR and CC are related to each other, an explanation of *CSR initiatives* from a broad perspective has been put forward (2.2.3). It indicates that CSR is the more academic term describing the social responsibilities business has to society, whereas CC is the more managerial term enacting concrete actions serving community-relations. Accordingly, CSR initiatives have been defined as actions that foster a socially-based purpose or a stakeholder group. Since CSR initiatives address a variety of stakeholders, such activities are meant to establish lasting stakeholder-relationships (2.3). In this respect it has been mentioned that CSR initiatives must be communicated accurately. To arrive at the result that employees play a crucial role as stakeholder-group, firstly basic ideas of stakeholder theory and stakeholder-management have been delineated (2.3.1). According to Freeman's landmark-definition a stakeholder is considered as *any group or individual who can affect or is affected by the firm's objectives*. On that account, the three different views of stakeholder approaches by Donaldson/Preston have been mentioned, in particular the *descriptive*, the *instrumental*, and the *normative view*. Based on these three views stakeholder theory refers to a managerial imperative leading to stakeholder management. *Stakeholder management* can be differentiated by two approaches: *Strategic* stakeholder management aims at generating positive effects contributing to the overall firm's performance. On the contrary, *intrinsic* stakeholder management is understood as a moral commitment to treat stakeholders in a positive way. Then, secondly, in section 2.3.2 employees have been identified as a 'first-class-stakeholder'. Clarkson differentiates between primary and secondary stakeholders, whereas employees – as in many other classifications – fall into the group of primary stakeholders. This notion has been substantiated by reasons from the *firms'* and the *employees' perspective* as well as due to the angle of strategic and intrinsic stakeholder management. According to a study put forward by Carmeli and colleagues CSR initiatives help to build lasting relationships in terms of the employees' identification with firm.

3. Organisational Identification of Employees

Chapter 3 serves to examine the concept of OI. The purpose is to reveal a proper understanding of *what* OI is and *why* it has obtained such useful practical implications for both companies and individuals. Section 3.1 will start with a theoretical and conceptual framework: Firstly, early scientific approaches are sketched that depict the nature of identification itself and also in the context of organisations (3.1.1). Afterwards the well-known SIA is put forward, which prevails as the underlying theoretical framework in order to explain the concept of OI (3.1.2). Then, in section 3.2 the findings of the SIA are applied to the context of organisations. After defining OI as specific form of social identification (3.2.1), different conceptualisations in terms of dimensions and foci will be displayed (3.2.2). A model by Dutton and colleagues will illustrate in how far the identity and the image of organisations is associated with OI (3.2.3). Section 3.3 answers the question why OI is useful in many respects. Several reasons will be conducted from two different perspectives, one from the perspective of the company (3.3.1), and the other from the individual (3.3.2). Chapter 3 will close with summarising the most important aspects (3.4).

3.1   Theoretical and Conceptual Framework

3.1.1   The Emergence of the Concept of Organisational Identification

Among scientific literature the concept of OI is a relatively new concept, although it is related to terms such as identity or identification which were frequently discussed beforehand in the fields of psychology, sociology or social psychology.[100] Early concepts of OI have primarily discussed identification merely in a work-related context in terms of job involvement or the intention of an employee to resign.[101] One of the first to introduce a concept has been Foote, who posits that human beings tend to identify themselves to so called "fellow in groups"[102]. According to Foote, group categorisations evoke certain behaviours and result into forms of commitment:

> "These categorizations of experience motivate behaviour through the necessary commitment of individuals in all situations."[103]

---

[100] Sea Riketta 2005: 360; Böhm 2008: 29.
[101] See Van Dick 2004: 1.
[102] Foote 1951: 21.
[103] Ibid. Interestingly Foote puts forward that individuals as group members can be motivated in their actions in the sense of a group. This idea will be emphasised through the elaboration of the SIA in Section (3.1.2). Sea also for the following Böhm 2008: 30ff.

Twenty years later Brown has proposed an empirical study on identification against the background of organisations. This study relies on the understanding that identification in the context of individuals and organisations is a part of the individuals' self-concept. On that score Brown has suggested a concept that contains four aspects of involvement: (1) The attraction to the organisation, (2) the consistency of organisational and individual goals, (3) loyalty, and (4) the reference of self to organisational membership.[104] Roughly at the same time Patchen advanced another concept of OI that comprises similarities with that of Brown. Patchen distinguishes three different components that contribute to a wider understanding of the concept: These are (1) the perception of shared characteristics with other group members, (2) a feeling of solidarity and belonging to the organisation and (3) the support of the organisational goals and policies.[105] Also Hall and colleagues underline correspondent to their study that OI is a concept by which the individual sees himself as integrated so that he incorporates the goals and values of the organisation into his own identity.[106]

Considering the different works which contributed into shaping the concept of OI it can be subsumed that a few authors among others dealt with this subject. Interestingly, apart from the various approaches, most attempts have several aspects in common, such as the idea that an organisational member links his organisational membership to his self-concept or the feeling of loyalty and belonging.[107] Nonetheless it has been criticized that these concepts do not derive from a theoretical framework that embeds identification into an organisational context properly. This incoherence also resulted into the problem that it has often been confused with other closely related terms such as organisational commitment[108]. For that reason, the problem of a missing theoretical reference point has been solved by the emergence of the SIA.[109]

3.1.2 The Social Identity Approach as Theoretical Ground Work

The SIA[110] is a well-known theory from a socio-psychological perspective that has been developed mainly by Tajfel/Turner.[111] According to contemporary literature on OI the SIA serves as the most prevalent theory, since it is the foundation for all further developments within this

---

[104] See Brown 1969: 349. The concept of identification which Brown relied on was introduced by Kelman: "[…] identification is a self-defining response, set in a specific relationship" (Kelman 1958: 52).
[105] See Patchen 1970: 155.
[106] See Hall et al. 1970: 176f.
[107] See Riketta 2005: 360f; Böhm 2008: 31f. For reasons of simplification the present thesis solely makes use of masculine forms.
[108] The concept of organisational commitment is probably the closest to OI, since it is often mixed up or used in order to explain OI. Among others a frequently cited definition has been put forward by Mowday and colleagues who see in organisational commitment as "the relative strength of an individual's identification with, and involvement in a particular organization" (Mowday et al. 1982: 27). See also Rometsch 2008: 123; Böhm 2008: 47ff.
[109] See Ashforth/Mael 1989: 20; Van Dick: 2004: 1f.
[110] See for a general overview Haslam 2004: 18ff.
[111] For a fundamental understanding of the SIA see Tajfel 1978, 1981; Tajfel/Turner 1986; Turner 1975, 1978, 1985.

branch of research as well allowing fruitful applications to organisational behaviour.[112] Generally speaking the SIA is composed of the social identity theory (SIT) and the self-categorisation (SCT) theory which are to be presented in particular subsequently.

In the first instance SIT aims to explain the nature of inter-group conflicts and inter-group discriminations. The underlying question is why group-members tend to estimate their own group as better or even superior compared to other out-groups. To investigate this 'in-group bias' Tajfel and colleagues have run the so called 'minimal group studies'[113] which revealed the following:

> "[...] in-group bias is a remarkably omnipresent feature of intergroup relations [...]. In other words, the mere awareness of the presence of an out-group is sufficient to provoke intergroup competitive or discriminatory responses on the part of the in-group."[114]

Although cooperative strategies were made available, the test persons consciously deviated from their economic self-interest. Rather the leading motive in preferring the in-group was "to beat the out-group"[115]. This behaviour can be explained as individuals categorise (*categorization*) and define themselves as a member of a group.

> "[...] the essential criteria for group membership [...] that the individuals concerned define themselves and are defined by others as members of a group. We conceptualize a group in this sense, as a collection of individuals who perceive themselves to be members of the same social category, share some emotional involvement in this common definition of themselves, and achieve some degree of social consensus about the evaluation of their group and of their membership."[116]

Thus, any behaviour by a group member towards others is based on the individuals' identification of himself and others as associated to different social categories. Such social categories would be for instance organisational membership, gender, religion or age. Based on these social categories individuals are able to locate themselves within society which gives them stability and orientation. As a consequence, the stronger the identification with a social category, the more it is expected that the social category is linked to the self concept of an individual.[117] The sum of all these social identifications that individuals take into account to define themselves is called *social identity*:

---

[112] See Böhm 2008: 39.

[113] The design of the minimal group studies was the following: Test persons were separated into two groups. They were told to be divided by certain criteria but in fact they were randomly allocated to their groups. The experiment had two distinct parts. The first part was meant to establish an intergroup categorisation. So the test persons were brought together and were asked to estimate the number of dots flashed on a screen. The second part was designed to evaluate the effects of the group categorisation on the intergroup behaviour. Therefore, the randomly allocated groups were labelled after the two painters 'Kandinsky' and 'Klee' and were requested to deal with money which was represented by arbitrary code numbers. Even in such ,minimal' situations, it turned out that the preferred dominant strategy in allocating the money between test persons of the in-group and the out-group was the maximal differentiation in favour of the in-group. Although strategies were made available such as to gain a maximal profit for the in- and out-group, the subjects refused to allocate fair distributions. See Tajfel et al. 1971: 149ff.; Tajfel/Turner 1979: 38ff.; Tajfel/Turner 1986: 13; Haslam 2004: 17ff.

[114] Tajfel/Tuner 1986: 13.

[115] Haslam 2004: 18.

[116] Tajfel/Turner 1979: 40.

[117] "*Identification* with a group – the extent to which a group is valued and self-involving – is [...] one particularly factor which affects a person's readiness to use a given social category in order to define themselves [...]" (Haslam 2001: 52, emphasis in original).

"[...] [S]ocial identity will be understood a that *part* of an individual's self-concept which derives from his knowledge of his membership of a social group (or groups) together with the value and emotional significance to that membership."[118]

The notion behind this idea is that of the *self-concept*. Against the background of SIT it is assumed that the self-concept is comprised by two parts: the first is the *social identity* encompassing significant group classifications to which an individual perceives himself as belonging to a certain social category. On the contrary the second part is the *personal identity* which is displayed in all idiosyncratic characteristics of an individual, meaning e.g. bodily attributes, taste, intellectual capacities or interests.[119] Employing this as focal point, with regard to the analysis of social identities, two sociocognitive processes can be identified which are of importance: On the one hand, as just described, the process of group categorisations, on the other hand the pursuit of individuals to experience a feeling of *self-enhancement* by means of positive demarcations to other relevant groups.[120] Hence, it can be supposed that the social identity plays a significant role regarding the self-estimation and the self-consciousness of an individual. So if the social identity is very distinct and is seen by the individual in a positive manner, it has a direct impact on the self-confidence.[121]

On that score the SIT can be based on three general assumptions: (1) Individuals strive to maintain or enhance their self-esteem, (2) social groups or categories and the membership of them are linked with positive or negative connotations, so that the social identity is either positive or negative according to the evaluations of the individual, and (3) in order to preserve a positive social identity with reference to specific other groups an individual pursues social comparisons in terms of value-based attributes and characteristics. Positively discrepant comparisons between in-group and out-group generate high prestige and vice versa.[122]

---

[118] Tajfel 1978: 63, emphasis in original.
[119] See Turner 1982: 18; Ashforth/Mael 1989; 21; Haslam 2001: 31. It can be doubted that e.g. personal taste could be the result of a process of adjustment within social categories. Nevertheless this plays for the following a minor part. See also Rometsch 2008: 119.
[120] See Hogg/Terry 2001: 3f.; Pratt 1998: 187.
[121] See Hogg/Terry 2001: 4, Böhm 2008: 34. Acknowledging this, the test persons' behaviour of the minimal group studies becomes comprehensible due to the striving for a positive social identity.
[122] See Tajfel/Turner 1986: 16. "The aim of differentiation is to maintain or achieve superiority over an out-group on some dimensions. Any such act, therefore, is essentially competitive" (Tajfel/Turner 1979: 41). The differentiation process is subject to three different variables that influence these concrete social situations: (1) Individuals must *internalise* their group membership as a component of their self-concept and also feel as being a genuine member of the group. It is not sufficient that the other group-members define the individual as associated to the group. (2) Furthermore, the social *situation* is a crucial factor. Since individuals are members of many different social categories at the same time (man/woman, nationality, profession etc.) not all categories can be of the same significance for the self-concept. (3) Moreover, in-groups do not compare themselves with every available out-group. See Tajfel/Turner 1986: 16; Haslam 2004: 21f.; Böhm 2008: 35. In this respect Tajfel/Turner mention three different strategies that could help to alleviate such problems: (1) One strategy is the *individual mobility* that describes a behaviour which allows individuals to switch from one group to another in case they think the new group contributes to enhance their social identity. (2) Another strategy is called *social creativity*. Members of a group change the category to differentiate in order to elevate the status of the group. (3) A last strategy is the *social competition* that can be identified to overcome in- and out-group processes of differentiation. According to this strategy members of the in-group seek for a direct confrontation with the out-group to reverse the negative comparison.

Turner and colleagues have picked up the results of SIT and advanced the scientific research to the already mentioned SCT.[123] Thus, the fundamental achievement of SCT is that it explains when and why a specific social identity or a social category becomes notably salient. It is posited that individuals primarily create categories in situations when the members resemble each other at most and also when they differ most preferably to members of other categories.[124] So the relation between the social identity and intergroup behaviours is of a special interest. Turner's hypothesis states that the social identity depends on a cognitive mechanism "which seems to be 'switched on'" depending on the particular situation.[125] The psychological process that can be specified here is termed as *depersonalisation*. It refers to a process of self-stereotyping which means that "the self comes to be perceived as categorically interchangeable with other in group members"[126]. Individuals consequently perceive such social categories and groups not being represented by unique individuals, but rather by *stereotypes*. The underlying impetus for this can be seen in *uncertainty avoidance*. Such social categories and intergroup processes alleviate to individuals how to comprehend different situations in different contexts:

> "Self-categorization reduces uncertainty by transforming self-conception and assimilating self to a prototype that describes and prescribes perceptions, attitudes, feelings, and behaviours. [...] It is the prototype that actually reduces uncertainty."[127]

The overall criterion whether an individual categorises him- or herself to a group is answered by social categorisation theory with the term of *salience*. Depending on the particular context some categories become more salient than others.

To help illustrate when and why some categories are more salient than others, two criteria exist which reveal the circumstances: For one thing it is the *accessibility*, for another it is the *fit*.[128] Accessibility describes the disposition of an individual to accept a certain social category in terms of being committed to belong to a group, whereas the fit of a social categorisation is the degree to

---

[123] Sea Turner et al. 1987: 42ff.; Pratt 1998: 178ff.; Hogg/Terry 2000: 122ff. The reason for this was that SIT lacks a sound analysis of the cognitive processes associated with social identity salience.

[124] See Turner et al. 1987: 42. "[I]t will be useful to avoid confusion by pointing out that the theory to be presented [Self-Categorisation-Theory (LR)] is related to but not the same as the SIT of intergroup behaviour referred to earlier. The earlier analysis was specifically directed at the explanation of *intergroup* discrimination (in the absence of conflicts of interest) and its central psychological hypothesis is motivational (or cognitive-motivational) – that individuals seek to differentiate their own groups positively from others to achieve a positive social identity. The current theory, developed later, is focussed on the explanation not of a specific kind of group behaviour but of how individuals are able to act as group at all. The basic hypothesis is a cognitive (or socio-cognitive) elaboration of the nature of social identity as a higher order level of abstraction in the perception of self and others. Logically speaking, the current theory is more general and can be seen to include former as a derivation" (Turner et al. 1987: 42, emphasis in original).

[125] "In other words, we are hypothesizing that social identity is the cognitive mechanism which makes group behaviour possible" (Turner 1982: 21).

[126] Haslam 2004: 30.

[127] Hogg/Terry 2000: 124. In section 3.2.2 it will be outlined in detail why individuals have motives to categorise themselves to social categories and groups.

[128] See ibid: 125. "The category that best fits the field becomes salient in that context" (Hogg/Terry 2000: 125).

which it matches from the perspective of the subject to relevant features of reality.[129] In this respect Böhm summarises three aspects that make a category more salient: (1) In case the category is new and something special, (2) if the category is struggling with other relevant categories or groups, or (3) if the category is especially mentioned.[130]

3.2 The Social Identity Approach Applied to Organisations

3.2.1 Organisational Identification as Specific Form of Social Identification

Since the SIA is considered as a fundamental piece of ground work, it has motivated various social psychologists to adapt the findings to the context of organisations.[131] The membership within work organisations is probably one the most important group affiliations an individual obtains throughout his life, since individuals spend a huge amount of their lifetime at their workplace. Hence, a deeper understanding of the bases and elements of identification in organisational contexts is of a deep interest.[132]

A central role in bridging the SIA and OI has been developed by Ashforth/Mael.[133] Considering the deliberations of SIT, individuals define themselves by means of salient group membership (see section 3.1.2). The organisation, as a social category, is perceived as impersonating characteristics that are prototypical of the members or of the organisation.[134] Ashforth/Mael argue that this cognitive mechanism is considered as a form of social identification, which they clarify in particular as the perception of oneness and belongingness to an organisation.[135] Through social identification, the individual perceives him as psychologically intertwined with the group. It is also put forward that members share certain occurrences as a common destiny and experience successes and failures as if they were their own.[136] Against this background OI shall be defined as

> "[…] a specific form of social identification where the individual defines him or herself in terms of their membership in a particular organization"[137]

and is also seen as

> "the perception of oneness with or belongingness to some human aggregate."[138]

---

[129] See Haslam 2004: 34. Hereby two forms of fits are distinguished: the comparative fit and the normative fit. In terms of the comparative fit a person will define him- or herself according to a particular self-category to the extent that the differences between members of that category and others that are salient in another context. On contrary, the normative fit tries to explain that social category becomes more salient, when the perceived similarities and differences between the members of a category do not meet the prior expectations.

[130] See Böhm 2008: 38 and the cited literature.

[131] See for an overview Dutton et al. 1994: 239ff.; Pratt 1998: 175ff.; Haslam 2001: 34ff.

[132] See Van Dick et al. 2004a: 172.

[133] See Ashforth/Mael 1989: 21ff. Their work also addresses the scientific branch of organisational behaviour.

[134] See Ashforth/Mael 1995: 311f.

[135] Ashforth/Mael 1989: 21.

[136] See Mael/Ashforth 1992: 105f.

[137] Mael/Ashforth 1992: 105. See also Ashforth/Mael 1989: 21ff; Dutton et al. 1994: 239f.; Mael/Ashforth 1995: 105f.

[138] Ashforth/Mael 1989: 21.

Within the subsequent section the focus lays on discussing specific elements of the nature of OI due to demonstrating the multidimensionality of social identification in the existence of different dimensions and foci.

3.2.2 Dimensions and Foci

Following Van Dick and colleagues, it is considered to be useful to distinguish between different dimensions and different foci of OI.[139] The following will stick to this order and will present at first the dimensions and then the foci.

The distinct dimensions indicate further characteristics of identification in conjunction with organisations. Basically the dimensions directly built on the knowledge of SIT by Tajfel.[140] With reference to this definition Ellemers and colleagues derive three intra-psychological processes that put emphasis on the group-based social identity: (1) *Social categorisation*, which is a cognitive process helping the individual to organise his or her social environment, (2) *social comparison*, which gives meaning in terms of comparing the own group with other relevant out-groups, and (3) *social identification* as final process which is considered as the individual's emotional attachment with a particular group.[141] In contrast to Ashforth/Mael, who see in OI a purely cognitive process (see 3.2.1), the three different processes mark the foundation so that four dimensions of OI can be addressed:[142]

- Referring to Ashforth/Mael the *cognitive* dimension describes an individual's perception and verification being a member of a particular social category or group. This form of self-categorisation is dependent on the social context and is displayed in situations in which the membership to the in-group is highlighted due to comparisons to other relevant out-groups.[143]

- The *evaluative* dimension marks the process when characteristics of a particular group are evaluated and checked by the individual. The evaluation comprises both, what the individual recognises, and attributes that are ascribed to the group from outside.

- Another dimension is considered as *affective* or *emotional*. It indicates an individuals' evaluation of a group that is driven by emotional concerns.

---

[139] See Van Dick et al. 2004a: 174.
[140] See Tajfel 1978: 63; Van Dick 2004: 15f.; Böhm 2008: 41.
[141] See Ellemers et al. 2004: 462f.
[142] See Ashforth/Mael 1989: 21; Böhm 2008: 41f.
[143] See Ashforth/Mael 1989: 21ff.

- Finally, identification with a group might also flow into a *behavioural* dimension. It relates to the individuals' behaviour, which refers to an active advocacy for the goals and values of the in-group.[144]

It ought to be underlined that the chronological order of the different dimensions is not arbitrary. In terms of a psychological process the fundamental precondition for the emergence of identification is set by the cognitive dimension because it is inevitably necessary that a member of a group has to realize that he is member of a certain category. Once the subject has realised his membership of a social group, the other dimensions come into play. The evaluative and the affective dimension are possible to occur at the same time or one after the other. The behavioural dimension is usually the result of the other dimensions.[145]

Besides the classification of a multidimensional concept of identification in terms of dimensions, many authors also discussed another perspective to approach the construct of OI.[146] Basically it is derived from Turner's assumptions to SCT, which indicates that individuals categorise themselves on different levels such as the *personal level*, the *intermediate or group level*, or as a human being in comparison to other species on a *super ordinate level*.[147] Translated in terms of organisational contexts, various empirical studies by Van Dick and colleagues could successfully prove that OI can be differentiated into different foci of identification. Hence, an employee can identify himself according to the subsequent foci:

- With his own career,
- with different subunits within the organisation such as departments or work groups,
- with the organisation as a whole,
- and with the occupational group the individual belongs to.[148]

Such a differentiation becomes particularly important, when different behaviours result from the different foci. Someone who is highly identified with his own career will concentrate on those activities that foster his career with the most benefit. From a theoretical perspective the assumptions of SIT, in particular the *category fit* (see section 3.1.2), underlines this notion. The more sali-

---

[144] See Van Dick 2004: 15f.; Böhm 2008: 42. The conative dimension was introduced to scientific literature later on after several authors developed various multi-dimensional concepts of identification according to the other three dimensions. Especially the work of Jackson (2002) marked a decisive point because he summarised distinct approaches and presented on the basis of empirical research the existence of a conative dimension. To him this dimension can be characterised as some kind of common fate. Furthermore, the conative dimension also has a lot in common with the concept of organisational commitment. See also footnote 108.

[145] See Van Dick 2004: 15ff. Furthermore, Van Dick and colleagues suggest that also context and category salience have a deep impact on all four dimensions. See Van Dick et al. 2004b: 174; Böhm 2008: 42.

[146] See Riketta/Van Dick 2004: 491ff. "Many researchers have argued that this psychological bond, or attachment, should not be treated as a uni-dimensional concept but should instead be considered as consisting of multiple elements" (Riketta/Van Dick 2004: 491).

[147] See Turner et al. 1987: 42ff.

[148] See Van Dick et al. 2004a: 172; Van Dick et al. 2005: 274. It is conceivable that there are other foci, too. For instance research was done according to geographically dispersed organisations or leadership qualities.

ent a category becomes the more determinant it gets to the individual. So, one would expect that it provides direction to act according to the enhancement of the self-concept.[149]

Another recent study by Van Dick and colleagues suggests that in cases of high identification with the organisation, as well as with the work group, resultant job satisfaction and extra-role behaviour would be higher than in cases where employees identify strongly with one of the foci but only weakly with the other, or identify with none of the foci.[150]

3.2.3 Identity and Image of Organisations as Precondition for Organisational Identification

Another prevalent concept to approach OI that received great attention among literature of OI has been set up by Dutton and colleagues. They argue that the strength of a member's cognitive connection to his work company is derived from two images each member has of his organisation. These two images are introduced as the *perceived organisational identity* and the *construed external image*.[151] Subsequently, each construct will be sketched one by one, followed by presenting the conflation to Dutton's and colleague's concept.

The *first* image is the construct of the perceived organisational identity which is considered as what a particular organisational member believes to be the distinctive, central, and enduring characteristics of his organisation. This notion has its roots within the concept *organisational identity*. A precise demarcation of organisational identity compared to OI is relatively difficult, which implies the consequence of them frequently being mixed up.[152] Basically, the idea is employed that organisations have identities that have an impact in how far organisational members interpret issues as well as how they react toward them.[153] Albert/Whetten articulate an understanding of organisational identity that is frequently accepted in organisational literature and is considered as a main development in this scientific branch, because it includes most facets that encompass for what an

---

[149] See Ellemers et al. 1998: 717ff.; Haslam 2004: 34.

[150] See Van Dick et al. 2008: 396.

[151] See Dutton et al. 1994: 239; See also especially regarding the constructed external image Dutton/Dukerich 1991: 548. The two constructs originate from a very early identity-concept by Mead. To become an accepted player within society individuals gain an understanding of the so called 'generalised other'. It is understood as a general norm within a social setting or a social group. Through understanding this 'generalised other' human beings get acquainted with what behaviours are expected of them and what is appropriate in specific social settings. According to the individuals' self-concept Mead distinguishes between the 'I' and the 'me'. With the help of the 'me' past experiences with social settings are sorted from the interaction with the social environment. This part of the self-concept marks the objectivised part of the identity and is observed by the 'I', which is the subjective part of the identity. The 'I' is rather some kind of reflector that continuously struggles with the social setting. "The 'I' is the response of the organism to the attitude of the others; the 'me' is the organized set of attitudes of others which one himself assumes. The attitudes of the others constitute the organized 'me', and then one reacts toward that as an 'I'" (Mead 1934: 175).

[152] See Albert et al. 2000: 13. "[…] many identity theorists conflate the terms identity and identification, implicitly treating them as synonyms for one's sense of self (who I am). However, there is value in differentiating the terms" (Sluss/Ashforth 2007: 11).

[153] See Dutton/Dukerich 1991: 518. According to Albert/Whetten the concept of organisational identity complies two uses: For one thing it is to describe the nature of organisations by defining and characterising them in a scientific manner. For another thing it is a concept that organisations make use of in order to portray themselves. Both streams are subject of the following. See Albert/Whetten 1985: 263f.

organisation stands for its members.[154] Accordingly, an organisational identity refers to what its members believe what are the "central, distinctive, and an enduring aspects of the organization"[155]. These aspects are in particular the "core values, organizational culture, modes of performance, and products"[156]. Cole/Bruch conceive the specific features of such elements that characterise an organisation as *identity content*.[157] However, some authors question whether the content of an organisations' identity can be subsumed to generalised statements. Under these circumstances Gioia and colleagues argue that an organisations' identity may modify in the course of time, since environments quickly change and today's organisations are confronted with increased complexity in terms of effects evoked through globalisation. It is likely to happen that in contexts of such an atmosphere companies switch their core business areas overnight including products and processes. As a consequence members may perceive the organisations' inherent characteristics rather as a "fluid and unstable construct"[158] than as stable and enduring.[159] The core assumption is that people obtain a sense of membership in a social category which shapes their self-concepts within a process where the individual's identity becomes psychologically intertwined with the organization's identity (see 3.1.2). Therefore, the perceived organisational identity shapes the strength of one's identification with an organisation.[160]

> "When organizational identification is strong, a member's self-concept has incorporated a large part of what he or she believes is distinctive, central, and enduring about the organization into what he or she believes is distinctive, central, and enduring about him- or herself."[161]

The *second* image in the concept of Dutton and colleagues is the so called *construed external image*, which puts more emphasis on the organisation's environment. Whereas the perceived organisational identity is a member's assessment of the organisation's nature, the construed external image describes the member's belief what outsiders think of his organisation. Insofar it is seen as some kind of powerful mirror that reflects how the organisation's characteristics approach the outside world.[162] Origins of this idea are to be found within the concept of organisational image which has been subject of many different conceptualisations and which was initially coined by marketing literature.[163] The construed external image relies on the fact that feelings and beliefs

---

[154] See Dukerich et al. 2002: 509. Nevertheless Gioia identifies three main streams in organisational literature. These "three lenses for understanding organizational identity" (Gioia 1998: 25) are the functionalist lens, the interpretive lens, and the postmodern lens. See for further details and a discussion on the lenses Gioia 1998: 25ff.
[155] Albert/Whetten 1985: 265.
[156] Ibid: 265.
[157] See Cole/Bruch 2006: 587.
[158] Gioia et al. 2000: 63.
[159] See Ibid: 63ff.; Böhm 2008: 57.
[160] See Cole/Bruch 2006: 585.
[161] Dutton et al. 1994: 242. "Organizational identification [...] occurs when members adopt the defining characteristics of the organization as defining characteristics for themselves" (Dutton et al. 1994: 242).
[162] See Dutton et al. 1994: 239 and 248f.
[163] See for a general overview of different conceptualizations Gioia et al. 2000: 65.

about an organisation merely exist in the perception of its audience.[164] Drawing on several case studies Dutton and colleagues summarise their theoretical arguments and empirical findings of the two images to the following hypotheses:

- The greater the attractiveness of the perceived organisational identity, the stronger an individual's OI.

- The greater the consistency between the attributes members take at hand to define themselves and the attributes used to define an organisational image, the stronger a member's identification.

- The greater the distinctiveness of an organisational image compared to other organisations, the stronger a person's OI.

- The more an organisational image enhances a member's self-esteem, the stronger the individuals' OI.[165]

The subsequent figure depicts the conflation between the perceived organisational identity, the construed external image and OI:

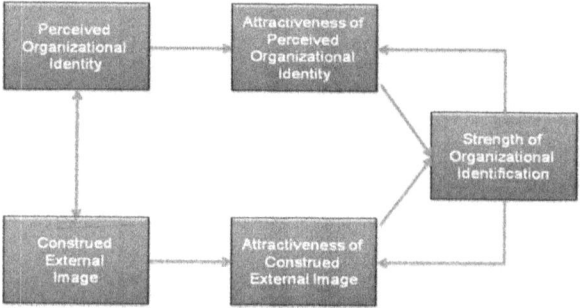

Figure 2: Linking Perceived Organisational Identity and Construed External Image To Strength of Organisational Identification. Source: Dutton et al. 1994: 253. Modified following Van Dick 2004: 53.[166]

According to this concept, the perceived organisational identity and the construed external image have a huge impact in on the strength of the employees' identification with his company. Referring to the double arrow between the perceived organisational identity and the construed external image Van Dick indicates that these two are not independent from each other. An employee,

---

[164] "[A]n organization's image describes attributes members believe people outside the organization use to distinguish it. [...] An organization's image matters greatly to its members because it represents members' best guesses at what characteristics others are likely to ascribe to them because of their organizational affiliation" (Dutton/Dukerich 1991: 547f.). See also Bernstein as cited in Abratt 1989: 68. On contrary, researchers from the field of organisational behaviour argued that the image is created through internal processes and internal perceptions. See Hatch/Schultz 1997: 358. "The organizational literature, in contrast to marketing, focuses almost exclusively on internal issues related to image" (Hatch/Schultz 1997: 358).
[165] See Dutton et al. 1994: 244ff. See also for a proper summarisation of the hypotheses Van Dick 2004: 52.
[166] Following Van Dick, the figure is a simplified version of the original model by Dutton and colleagues. With respect to the present topic it is sufficient in order to explain the basic ideas in connection with CSR. See Van Dick 2004: 53f.

who perceives his firm as positively viewed from the outside world, will also perceive the organisational identity in a more positive light and vice versa.[167]

3.3 The Significance for Companies and Individuals

3.3.1 Reasoning for the Interest in Organisational Identification by Companies

In the following several reasons will be outlined in order to underline the high significance OI comprises within the working world, since the degree to which an employee identifies with his organisation has positive consequences for both the organisation and the individual himself.[168]

Generally speaking, various reasons can be put forward why companies have a deep interest that employees build strong bonds of identification with their organisation. Within scientific literature authors recently identified the high relevance for the entire business world.

First of all, numerous researches on the effects of OI indicate positive effects for the company in terms of *efficiency* and *productivity*. Employees identified with their organisation reveal a better job performance, a higher commitment and a significant increase in cooperative behaviour.[169] Such behaviour is known to literature as *organisational citizenship behaviour* (OCB). According to Organ, OCB is considered as extra-role behaviour that is non-rewarded and contributes to the effective, beneficial functioning of an organisation. This form of voluntary conduct is usually not part of the contractual agreement between the employer and the employee and reflects a mutual sense of duty by the individual.[170]

Another study by Van Dick and colleagues rather focuses on the impact OI has on the fluctuation of employees. This study found out that strong OI feeds into *job satisfaction*, which in turn leads to low *turnover intention*.[171] Turnover is a major problem for many companies, since it is extremely costly, especially referred to jobs which require higher education and extensive job train-

---

[167] See Ibid. Van Dick also mentions the case of nationalists who are proud of their country, because it is seen negatively by other nations.
[168] See Böhm 2008: 15. There are several authors who did research on the link between OI and its effects for the individual as well for organisations. See Meyer/Allen 1997: 4ff.; Van Dick 2004: 7ff.; Riketta 2005: 360ff.; Riketta/Van Dick 2005: 491ff. The way employees are viewed as part of a business enterprise has undergone an evolutionary process towards the understanding of precious human resources: "Der Schwerpunkt der Managementaufgabe verlagert sich damit vom Bemühen um Ökonomisch-Technische zur Ökonomisch-Sozial-Humanen Rationalität. Damit gewinnen die Humanressourcen als langfristig zu schaffendes und weiterzuentwickelndes Erfolgspotential einen zentralen Stellenwert für die Überlebens- und Entwicklungsfähigkeit einer Unternehmung" (Bleicher 1991: 26, German).
[169] See Bhattacharya et al. 1995: 47ff.; Mael/Ashforth 1995: 314f.; Van Dick 2004: 8; Böhm 2008: 15. This aspect can also be underlined with reference to the SIT: "[…] as a form of social identity, shared organizational identity is a basis not only for people to perceive and interpret their world in similar ways, but also for processes of mutual social influence which allow them to coordinate (and *expect* to coordinate) their behaviour in ways that lead to concerted social action and collective products" (Haslam et al. 2003: 364, emphasis in original).
[170] See Organ 1988; Van Dick et al. 2006: 284; Organ et al. 2006. Organ and colleagues define OCB the following: "Individual behavior that is discretionary, not directly or explicitly recognized by the formal reward system, and in the aggregate promotes the efficient and effective functioning of the organization" (Organ et al. 2006: 3).
[171] See Van Dick et al. 2004a: 351f.; Another study by Cole/Bruch comes to similar results. See Cole/Bruch 2006: 589.

ing.[172] The fact that employees feel strong bonds in terms of identification can not be considered as something taken for granted. A study published by the public opinion research company Gallup indicates that almost 88% of German employees do not feel constrained to their employer. They estimate the direct and indirect costs firms have to bear is approximately 88-92 billion € per year.[173] Having this in focus, Wienröder argues that the entire understanding of the working world has shifted. Job change rates have increased tremendously so the traditional image of the life-long employer as it was still common in the 20th century has vanished.[174] Particularly in the wake of a large increase in cross-border M&A-activities new forms of organisational change can be observed. Therefore, one could argue that OI could be hindering in terms of having difficulties to adjust with new organisational forms.[175]

This leads to another crucial reason which can be seen in the *skills* and *knowledge* employees occupy. The current economy is vigorously coined by the existence and development of knowledge. In the first place the employee himself is in need of profound knowledge and skills in order to cope with continuously changing organisations. As the organisational environment is subject to quick changes, employees play a major role determining the success of companies. But also, as high competitive markets require employees that undertake complex tasks, the human capital of a company is inevitable to dispense. According to Drucker the competitiveness of European and US companies is determined through their knowledge resources in order to develop and produce high tech products.[176] This applies specifically against the background of demographic changes as the structure of the working population will shift towards less well-educated employees.[177] Thus, since the building up of knowledge is lengthy and expensive, long-term bonds with employees are crucial success factors for companies.[178]

Furthermore, Van Dick also refers to an environment in which companies depict themselves as dynamic and multifaceted, there is high need of employees that not only represent, but rather *impersonate* the company. In particular with respect to processes of organisational change, it is

---

[172] See Van Dick et al 2004a: 351. For instance, a study by Argote and colleagues found out that groups with turnover produced significantly less products that those without turnover. See Argote et al. 1995: 512f.
[173] See Gallup 2005.
[174] See Wienröder 2006: 21.
[175] See Deloitte 2007: 34f. for further details on the increase of cross-border M&A activities. The process of adjustment goes also along with findings regarding organisational culture and M&A-activities. It is argued that the degree how strong a culture is recognised by employees plays an important role during the process of adjustment to new organisational forms. See for further reading Schein 1991: 37; Forstmann 1994: 67ff.
[176] See Drucker 2002: 12f.
[177] See Strack et al. 2008: 36.
[178] See Van Dick 2004: 9; Böhm 2008: 16.

important that such core members have a psychologically strong bond to the company, so that they are willing to precede working in a fruitful manner for the company.[179]

Another aspect which goes along with new forms of organisational change is that modern organisations tend to reduce hierarchical structures. As a consequence employees are in charge to take care of themselves which implies a high degree of *autonomy* and *self-responsibility*. Employees who strongly identify with their organisation will not take advantage of their new freedom in favour of their self-interest. They will rather be concerned about the companies' current issues and stand up for the purposes of the firm.[180]

3.3.2 Reasoning for the Interest in Organisational Identification by Individuals

When needs come into play, literature mostly refers to the hierarchy of needs by the clinic psychologist Maslow. Maslow's hierarchy of needs is often displayed as pyramid which consists of five levels: 1) physiological needs, 2) safety needs, 3) social needs, 4) Esteem, and 5) self-actualisation. Starting from the hypothesis of deficiency, it is expected that lower needs must be met fist. Once they are fulfilled individuals seek to satisfy needs on a higher level.[181] In terms of identification it is argued that individuals benefit from OI as it satisfies basic needs so that identification is seen "as a basic human function"[182]. In this respect literature identifies four basic human needs that can be put forward being fulfilled by identification. In particular these are safety needs, affiliation needs, self-enhancement needs and holistic needs.[183]

The *need for safety* is a very strong need for human beings. Often this need accrues from feelings of uncertainty and vulnerability.[184] In order to overcome such a state, individuals pursue the desire for physical and psychological safety.[185] According to the scientific branch of personality development it is referred that individuals aspire to gain control over their environment, which can be achieved by means of experiencing own competences (self-efficacy) and repetitive, predictable patterns (self-continuity).[186] The feeling of being safe can moreover be created through single persons. Correspondent to an empirical study by Bulis/Bach it is indicated that identification is likely to appear during specific turning points in a mentor-protégé relationship. The protégés'

---

[179] See Van Dick 2004: 8. Van Dick also differentiates between long-term and short-term employees of a company. He mentions a study by Van Dyne/Ang (1998) which suggests employees who only work for a company a short period of time not necessarily feel less compared to those employees who work on long-term basis.
[180] See Van Dick 2004: 8; Böhm 2008: 15f.
[181] See Maslow 1943: 370-296; Berthel/Becker 2003: 21.
[182] Pratt 1998: 181.
[183] See for a general overview Ibid: 180ff.; Van Dick 2004: 10ff.; Böhm 2008: 17. It should be noted that the distinct four needs are also interlinked in their mechanism as well. For instance, an individual can experience the need of affiliation to an organisation through self-enhancement. It should be noted that originally Pratt does not directly relate to identification in terms of organisations. Later, other authors like Van Dick or Böhm mention the needs referred to OI.
[184] See Van Dick 2004: 11.
[185] See Pratt 1998: 182.
[186] See Erez/Earley 1993: 28ff.

identification with his mentor is fortified, since he asks for advice in order to overcome his feelings of uncertainty.[187]

The desire for safety can also be applied to organisations. Accordingly, being a member of a group and identifying with it serves to reduce feelings of uncertainty and vulnerability. As long as individuals have the opportunity to categorise themselves to a group, they do not obtain the feeling of being alone and arrive at the conclusion of having others behind them.[188] Ashforth/Mael suggest that whenever external groups exert threats on the in-group, this will result into stronger identification by the in-group members.[189] This aspect could be observed in the context of M&A-activities, that is, when employees suddenly feel constrained to their 'old' company.[190] Then again, Nair/Pratt describe cases when employees unexpectedly get the urge to become part of the 'new' company, although this was once the obnoxious business rival. Such forms of identification may be explained through the lack of alternatives in order to survive radical change in the working environment.[191]

Another frequently mentioned need concerns the *need for belonging and affiliation*, since liking a person or a group is a prevalent motivating force for identification.[192] In this respect Aronson notes that identification "puts us in a satisfying relationship to the person or persons with whom we are identifying"[193]. Therefore, this kind of identification is associated to individuals' social needs as it was already suggested by Ashforth/Mael's view of OI outlined above.[194]

Moreover, the feeling of affiliation is fundamental in the context of OI, because it enables individuals to flee from a status of social isolation. Being identified with an organisation it can be considered as a response to separateness and loneliness. On that score Cheney states, "as an individual response to the divisions of society, a person acts to identity with some target(s)"[195].

Again, in the light of a continuously changing business environment as well as more frequent specialisation and the division of labour (see section 3.3.1), employees are often overwhelmed by the task to cope with such developments. Thus, OI can be seen as a remedy for individuals to overcome such estrangements.[196]

---

[187] See Bullis/Bach 1989: 199ff.
[188] See section 3.1.2 for SCT.
[189] See Ashforth/Mael 1989: 25.
[190] See Van Dick 2004: 10.
[191] See Nair/Pratt 1997 as cited in Pratt 1998: 182. This form of identification reminds also to well-known case of the so called 'Stockholm effect', whereas the kidnap victim suddenly identifies with the kidnapper. By means of converging at the kidnapper, the kidnap victim tries to overcome his feelings of uncertainty and vulnerability by identifying with the same targets of the kidnapper.
[192] See Ashforth/Mael 1989: 21.
[193] Aronson 1992: 34. According to this, Böhm draws an analogy to sports. Fans identify with a distinct team or club and express their belonging through clothes, slogans and some sort of corporate behaviour. See Böhm 2008: 71.
[194] See section 3.2.1; Ashforth/Mael 1989: 21.
[195] Cheney 1983: 145.
[196] See Pratt 1998: 183.

The desire of individuals for *self-enhancement* has already been discussed in section 3.1.2 in connection with the SIA. Individuals seek to have a self-concept, which is comprised by the personal and social identity, which is viewed by themselves in a positive light. Accordingly, identification is driven by the urge to increase self-worth and self-enhancement.[197]

For one thing, this can be achieved on an interpersonal level through the individuals' identification with another person, who is highly respected and is held in high esteem. While copying the behaviour of an admired person, individuals try to enhance their sense of self-worth.[198]

For another thing, a large part of the self-esteem is derived from social interaction as e.g. by means of praise or recognition. Hence, when an individual perceives himself as being a member of a group and experiences this through forms of social interaction and mutual acknowledgment, identification with this social category is likely to influence their self-esteem positively.[199]

With reference to OI Dutton and colleagues underline an organisations' attractive image lets the identification of employees increase:

> "[…] organizational membership can confer positive attributes on its members, and people may feel proud to belong to an organization that is believed to have socially valued characteristics."[200]

Employees identified with their organisation, project the positive attributes to themselves in order to experience their self-concept as unique and distinctive.[201]

Finally, a last need that can be identified is the desire for *holistic needs*. It means that individuals seek to identify with an organisation in order to find meaning or some kind of purpose in their lives.[202] Concerning the causes for such desires, similar reasons are put forward compared to the need for affiliation. Rapidly changing market environments, global competition, new organisational forms and an instable work-life-balance are developments that can be made responsible for a strong demand for meaning. Since individuals recognise that their lives are more fragmented, they seek as a result to find a deeper meaning which contributes to reorder or even simplify their lives.[203]

Organisations that consistently pursue a particular vision or a worldview may produce relief as they are successful in creating identification so that individuals feel more complete and integrated. Especially, this accounts to organisations that obtain a remarkable vision or a specific philosophy, which in some ways also reminds to some sort of religious ideas.

---

[197] See Tajfel/Turner 1986: 16; Hogg/Terry 2001: 3f.; Pratt 1989: 183.
[198] See Erez/Earley 1993 28.
[199] See Van Dick 2004: 11.
[200] Dutton et al. 1994: 240. More on that subject will be presented later in section 4.2.3.
[201] See Pratt 1998: 183.
[202] See Ibid.
[203] See Ibid; Van Dick 2004: 12; Böhm 2008: 72.

At the same time the search for meaning can also be fostered by a coherent strategy or an attractive image.[204] The logic behind that is constituted through the humans' imperfection, which individuals try to compensate by being a member in an organisation that conveys attributes associated with meaning to them.[205] Thus, individuals are in search of an organisation "where they can enact one's set of deeply held personal values"[206].

3.4   Intermediate Result

The preceding chapter basically dealt with the concept of OI and tried to outline *what* is understood by this concept and *why* it is such a useful concept for both companies and individuals. Section 3.1 served to sketch the theoretical and conceptual framework of OI. Early approaches, for instance put forward by Foote, Brown or Patchen, have tried to characterise identification in a work-related context. Their findings on identification indicate that members of an organisation link their membership to their self-concept and that they feel some sort of attraction and belonging (3.1.1). Since the early approaches faced a missing theoretical framework, the socio-psychological *SIA* by Tajfel/Turner was introduced in section 3.1.2. The first component of the SIA approach is the *SIT*. It indicates that individuals categorise themselves to social categories (*categorisation*), which in turn evokes the urge to experience a feeling of *self-enhancement* by means of positive demarcations to other relevant out-groups. Based on SIT, the second component of the SIA, *social categorisation theory*, broadens the understanding in terms of explaining when and why a specific social category becomes more salient to individuals. Accordingly, individuals primarily create categories in situations when the members resemble each other at most and also when they differ most preferably to members of others categories. To highlight when and why some social categories become more salient, the two criteria of *accessibility* and *fit* were presented. Afterwards, the findings of the SIA were applied to the context of organisations so that the analysis could focus on OI (3.2). Referring to Ashforth/Mael OI was defined as "specific form of social identification" and as "the perception of oneness with or belongingness" to an organisation (3.2.1). Then, OI was systematised according to different *dimensions* and different *foci* (3.2.2). In terms of the dimensions four types could be located that are based on intra-psychological processes. In particular there is a *cognitive*, an *evaluative*, an *affective*, and a *behavioural* dimension. Moreover, OI can also be differentiated into different foci. An employee can therefore identify with his own *career*, with different *subunits* within the organisation, with the *organisation as a whole*, and with the *occupational group* the individual belongs to. In section 3.2.3 a well-known concept by Dutton and colleagues has been introduced which is based on two main images. The *perceived organisational identity*

---

[204] See Van Dick 2004: 12.
[205] See Pratt 1998: 184.
[206] Neck/Milliman 1994: 9.

is the members' assessment of the organisation's characteristics, whereas the *construed external image* describes the member's belief what outsiders think of his organisation. Both images can have a huge impact on the strength of the employees' identification with his company.

Section 3.3 was set up in order to outline the huge significance of OI for both companies and individuals. Regarding the utility companies benefit from OI by more *efficiency* and *productivity* due to *OCB* of employees. In addition, a higher *job satisfaction* generates less *turnover intentions*, which becomes very important, since companies in complex environments have a deep interest to keep their employees in order not to give away strong resources in terms of *skills* and *knowledge*. Furthermore, today's companies need identified employees that impersonate the companies' core images and are able to handle high degrees of *autonomy* and *self-responsibility* on behalf of the firm. (3.3.1) Concerning the interest in OI by individuals, identification satisfies basic human needs such as the need for *safety*, *affiliation*, *self-enhancement* and *holism* (3.3.2).

4. Corporate Social Responsibility & Organisational Identification: To Which Extent Do CSR Initiatives Achieve Organisational Identification?

The purpose of chapter 4 is to bridge chapters 2 and 3 in order to provide insights to the core question: To which extent do CSR initiatives achieve OI of employees?

In the first place it is necessary to reveal an understanding of how OI emerges. Accordingly, the functional chain will be sketched in section 4.1, which will serve as the underlying model to explain the correlation between CSR and OI. Then, in section 4.2 three different approaches will be presented that exist among scientific literature on how (organisational) identification emerges. In particular these are the processes of affinity (4.2.1), emulation (4.2.2), and categorisation & self-enhancement (4.2.3). Drawing upon the three different processes, the entire functional chain will be reconstructed in terms of discussing the link between CSR and OI (4.3). In addition to the theoretical reconstruction, an overview of the status of scientific literature and practice-oriented studies will be displayed. Finally, important aspects are summarised and some deliberations by the author are reflected upon (4.4).

4.1 Functional Chain of Organisational Identification

With reference to the previous chapter, OI has been examined according to *what* it is and *why* it is considerably relevant for both the individual and for companies. In the present section the focus will lay on *how* OI emerges. Since it allows valuable insights to what extent CSR initiatives could be utilized to achieve identification, dealing with processes of the emergence of OI is very substantial.

In the first instance the following will rather concentrate on an abstract three-step-procedure of the functional chain. For that purpose we distinguish between the input, the processes and the outcome. The input (1) is also known as the driver or the antecedent. In the sense of the present paper the input is supposed to be the CSR initiatives. Such a driver triggers off the processes in the second step. These processes (2) that let OI appear are those of affinity, emulation, and categorisation and self-enhancement, which will be presented in detail within this section. Finally, the outcome (3) is the achievement of OI.[207] Following this logic, the subsequent figure visualizes the entire functional chain:

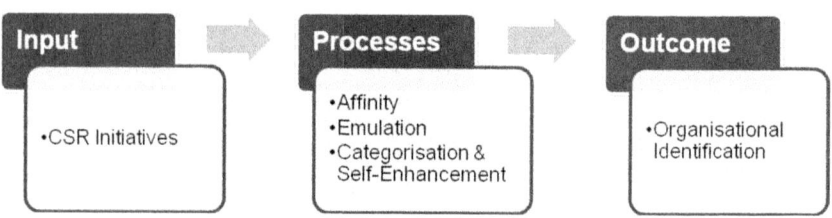

Figure 3: Functional Chain for the Emergence of Organisational Identification.
Source: Author's diagram modified following Bhattacharya et al. 2008: 40; Böhm 2008: 107.

To trace the functional chain of achieving OI, it is important to distinguish between the three processes and the driver. Whereas the processes solely describe how and why identification develops, the drivers operate to trigger off and amplify identification, which means they impact on the processes and have the ability to intensify them, unless they do not serve as a replacement for the processes of emergence themselves. Thus, the drivers on its own do not cause the outcome in terms of OI.[208]

4.2   Processes of the Emergence for Organisational Identification

Referring to scientific literature many suggestions have been put forward to describe processes how OI emerges.[209] Nonetheless a commonly accepted explanation has not been presented so that different approaches are prevalent. In this context Böhm summarises three major approaches: *affinity, emulation* as well as *categorisation and self-enhancement*.[210]

4.2.1   Affinity

Following this paradigm, OI emerges through *affinity*. An individual identifies with an organisation whenever his values consistently match the values the organisation represents. For instance, an ecologically sensitive person would rather identify with an employer that advocates for sustainable products and services than with a company that operates in the chemical industry.[211]

---

[207] See Bhattacharya et al. 2008: 40.
[208] See Böhm 2008: 69 and 107.
[209] See among others Ashforth/Mael 1989: 21ff.; Dutton et al. 1994: 239ff.; Pratt 1998: 178ff. as well as Haslam 2004: 67ff.
[210] See Böhm 2008: 73ff. in the following for the development of OI.
[211] See Böhm 2008: 74.

Hence, individuals are able to recognise parts of their own identity within the identity of the organisation:

> "When they [the employees (LR)] identify strongly with the organization, the attributes they use to define the organization also define them."[212]

Accordingly, someone will rather identify with an organisation that shares the same values and beliefs. This notion is also highlighted by Shamir, who states that a congruently perceived identity of the organisation offers more room for individuals to express themselves in a more salient way rather than hide the contents of their self-concept.[213] In order to maintain this integrity, individuals want to act authentically, expressing their own personal characteristics they think they have. In addition, employees, who work for a company that matches their values and beliefs, reside in an environment that gives them the opportunity to openly state their opinion.[214]

The idea of similar identities between personal and organisational values can also be found in earlier works regarding the so called 'person-organisation fit'. The results of associated studies suggest that greater person-organisation fit conducted into attitudes and behaviours consistent with stronger OI so that members of an organisation establish enormous bonding forces with their organisation.[215] These findings were later developed to the model already outlined in section 3.2.3 by Dutton and colleagues.[216]

Relating to concrete business processes personal characteristics, as for instance the values or opinions of an individual, could give a helpful direction in how far applicants bring along the prerequisites to generate OI as long as the company knows its own values which they represent in- and externally.[217]

4.2.2 Emulation

Another form of the emergence of OI takes place through *emulation*, whereas the values of an organisation are gradually internalised by the employee. A congruency of values and beliefs that already exists beforehand, as it has been put forward in terms of affinity, is according to this pro-

---

[212] Dutton et al. 1994: 239.

[213] See Shamir et al. 1993: 580. "Humans are not only pragmatic and goal oriented but also self-expressive" (Shamir et al. 1993: 580). Dutton and colleagues refer to the well-known example of Nike. Nike encourages its employees to work out during working time. So employees, who are sports-mad, get the opportunity to burgeon themselves and therefore rather identify with Nike. See Dutton et al. 1994: 244.

[214] See Gecas 1982: 23f. "People are drawn to organizations in which they can express themselves rather than hide the contents of their self-concept" (Dutton et al. 1994: 245).

[215] See Chatman 1989: 339ff. "Person-organization fit is defined here as the congruence between the norms and values of organizations and the values of persons" (Chatman 1989: 339).

[216] See section 3.2.3; Dutton et al. 1994: 239ff.; Dutton/Dukerich 1991: 547ff. Dutton/Dukerich refer to the following: "An organization's image describes attributes members believe people outside the organization use to distinguish it. [...] An organization's image matters greatly to its members because it represents members' best guesses at what characteristics others are likely to ascribe to them because of their organizational affiliation" (Dutton/Dukerich 1991: 548).

[217] See Mael/Ashforth 1995: 328f. One example that can be mentioned here, is that students who achieve excellent grades at university, rather identify with an organisation that claims values such as excellence or the commitment to high performance. See Böhm 2008: 75.

cess not necessary. Rather the defining attributes of the organisation adapt to the individual in the course of time. Thus, it suggests itself that the duration an individual belongs to an organisation positively correlates to higher OI.[218] Furthermore, Hogg and colleagues have introduced another explanation of emulation with the help of identity theory that sets out to explain individuals' role-related behaviours in terms of the reciprocal interactions between the self and society. Such role identities are self-definitions that subjects apply to themselves through a process of labelling as a member of a particular social category. From this it follows that for the emergence of identification within organisations individuals occupy certain roles, or role identities, and also impersonate them.[219] Closely related to this idea is the construct of *socialisation*, which is considered as "the process by which an individual acquires the social knowledge and skills necessary to assume an organizational role"[220]. As such, the process of socialisation concentrates on how individuals learn the values, beliefs, behaviours, skills necessary to fulfil their roles and functions effectively.[221] So in terms of the context of organisations, individuals adapt and also lay claim on the values and norms of the organisation. But, in case individuals suddenly occupy a different role within the organisation, the intensity of their OI may convert. This appears to happen, for instance, when an employee climbs up the hierarchy in the company, since he is confronted with a completely new role and as a consequence with new processes of socialisation.[222]

Moreover, it is argued that *communication* plays a central role in terms of the employees' willingness to identify with their organisation. According to Smidts and colleagues this applies to both the content of the communication, and also to the communication climate. Especially a positive communication climate has huge impact on the members' identification, since it reveals whether the member is accepted as a valued co-worker within the organisation.[223]

4.2.3 Categorisation and Self-Enhancement

The last approach to explain the emergence of OI builds on the findings of the SIA (see 3.1.2). On that score Böhm summarises in total seven mechanisms, which explain the emergence or non-emergence of OI. The first four mechanisms refer to the categorisation as a group member

---

[218] See Bhattacharya et al. 1995: 47ff.; Mael/Ashforth 1992: 116f.

[219] See Hogg et al. 1995: 255ff. Hogg and colleagues put emphasis on the fact that identity theory should not be confounded with SIT (see section 3.1.2). "Identity theory is principally a micro sociological theory that sets out to explain individuals' role-related behaviours, while social identity theory is a psychological theory that sets out to explain group processes and intergroup relations" (Hogg et al. 1995: 255).

[220] Van Maanen/Schein 1979: 211. The concept of socialisation is derived from sociology and refers to the adjustment process of an individual within a social environment.

[221] See Ashforth/Saks 1996: 149.

[222] See Hogg et al. 1995: 256. "Variation in self-concepts is due to the different roles that people occupy" (Hogg et al. 1995: 256).

[223] See Smidts et al. 2001: 1051. See also concerning the link between communication climate and the employees' willingness to identify with a company one of the first studies Welsch/LaVan 1981: 1086f.

and the last three correspond to the self-enhancement of the self-esteem by being a member of a certain group.[224]

(1) OI is more likely to occur in those organisations that are perceived as *distinctive* and *unique*. It allows its members a clear demarcation between the own organisation (in-group) and external organisations (out-group) so that are clear-cut categorisation is made possible, which in turn lets identification increase.[225]

(2) OI is also more likely to appear, when the *differences* to the external organisation become *apparent* and *salient*. Consequently, the attributes of the own organisation get more present, which lets identification grow. The other way round identification with the own organisation might lessen, since merely characteristics of the in-group are perceived salient as emphasis shifts to personal identities.

(3) OI develops more slowly, when the distinct members of the organisation are too *heterogeneous* and enter into *intra-organisational competition*. That way, inequalities are accentuated and reduced cohesion within the organisation is the consequence.

(4) Another difficulty to evoke OI emerges, when members of the in-group perceive other out-group members as too similar. Due to abstract identities, too much *homogeneity between organisations* affects the members' identification negatively.[226]

(5) OI is likely to be associated with the *prestige* of the organisation. Individuals often cognitively identify themselves with a winner that is popular.[227]

(6) In the same way a related factor increases OI, when the organisation is perceived with an *attractive* and *positive image*.[228]

(7) Finally, the perceived organisational identity also affects the way OI can be created. Attractive identities are represented through certain values that in-group members can assign to their self-concept.[229]

---

[224] See Böhm 2008: 76ff. Moreover, see for the following Pratt 1998: 184ff.; Ashforth/Mael 1989: 24ff. Regarding the mechanisms associated with self-enhancement is based on the assumption that organisations, which are positively perceived by their members and their environment, evoke distinctive OI compared to those which are perceived less positive.

[225] "Distinctiveness serves to separate 'figure from ground', differentiating the group from others and providing a unique identity" (Ashforth/Mael 1989: 24, emphasis in original).

[226] For instance, the presence of females in a male-dominated group induces males to exaggerate perceived masculine traits and differences between the sexes. See Ashforth/Mael 1989: 25.

[227] Again the example of a prestigious soccer club can be put forward. See Böhm 2008: 36.

[228] This aspect particularly refers to construed external image presented above (3.2.3). See Dutton et al. 1994: 248f.

[229] Ibid: 244ff. Such values could be e.g. power, excellence, or integrity. "When members associate with organizations that have an attractive perceived identity, it enhances their self-esteem as they acquire a more positive evaluation of self" (Ibid: 246).

With reference to the seven presented mechanisms not all of them could be separated accurately as some aspects apparently overlap. For instance, it is obvious that there are similarities regarding the emergence of OI by prestige (5) and a positive image (6).

Such similarities also apply to the two processes of emergence affinity and emulation. However, this is not supposed to suggest an either-or-decision. It is rather a matter of several accompanying mechanisms that contribute to the emergence of OI. That is, several processes may occur at the same time.[230]

4.3 To Which Extent Do CSR Initiatives Achieve Organisational Identification?: Theoretical Reconstruction, Recent Developments in Scientific Research and Discussion

Based on the functional chain presented in 4.1 the *theoretical reconstruction* proceeds by filling in CSR initiatives as driver to trigger off the processes for the emergence.

In terms of *affinity* the employee identifies with his firm whenever it shares the same values and beliefs. Since CSR initiatives represent the companies' values and beliefs (see section 2.2.3), they can be considered as a means to let the process of identification start, as long as the values communicated through CSR initiatives consistently match those of the employee. Accordingly, if an employee claims the value of academic excellence, a CSR initiative, which fosters educational institutions to achieve goals that are attached to this value, is very likely to be rewarded by the employee with more identification.

Based on *emulation* CSR initiatives could not be a driver for OI right from the beginning the employee is part of the company. To launch this process of identification, it is necessary that CSR initiatives are carried out consistently over a certain period of time, so that the employee is able to internalise the values represented through the initiatives in the course of time. Consequently, this requires an accurate communication which CSR initiatives the company is running and in what way they represent the companies' core characteristics.

The third process of *categorisation and self-enhancement* can also be activated by CSR initiatives. Referred to categorisation the CSR activity must be in its conception and realisation distinctive. Thus, with the effect of being demarcable to competitors (out-group), employees can categorise themselves to their company (in-group). A precondition is that those characteristics, which differ to the competitors, become salient to the employee. Therefore, the CSR initiative of the own firm shall not to be perceived by the employee as too homogeneous compared to those initiatives of other relevant competitors. According to self-enhancement the CSR activity should create a positive image to the outer environment so that employees feel elevated being a member of a socially highly valued company. This notion also refers to the construed external image of section 3.2.3 which is the member's belief what outsiders think of the organisation. Since the organisations'

---

[230] See Ibid; Böhm 2008: 79f.

identity can be represented through CSR initiatives, the other image of the model by Dutton and colleagues, the perceived organisational identity, finds as well its application as attractive identities affect the way OI emerges. Correspondingly, for instance an employee works at an automobile manufacturer and his company runs a CSR initiative fostering road safety, he will feel self-enhancement due to both images: Since road safety is socially highly valued, the construed external image will be positive. Equally, the perceived organisational identity will be linked with attractiveness as values are mediated such as responsibility, protection and solicitousness. Of course, the process can also direct into disidentification, if the construed external image and the organisational identity are attached with negative images.[231]

Referring to a *scientific review* of various studies some can be put forward which argue in the direction that the CSR of a company is positively linked to the OI of employees. The most relevant study aiming at this link has been published by Carmeli and colleagues. Their study has investigated the role of organisational performance labelled as the perceived CSR and the perceived CFP in evoking OI. The results indicate that both forms are attached to OI, whereas the perceived CSR has a larger effect on OI compared to the market and financial performance. The study has also shown that the OI in turn results into enhanced employees' work outcomes such as adjustment and the overall job performance.[232] A study by Marin/Ruiz demonstrates similar results from the perspective of the consumer. Insofar this is in indicator that the CSR of a firm could also help to let other stakeholder groups identify with a company.[233] Accordingly, this aspect could be picked-up as a starting point for further investigation on the link between CSR, OI and other stakeholders.

Moreover, some studies have focused on the positive effects that are created through the CSR of a firm. Here CSR directs not explicitly into OI, but it is advanced as driver to evoke attractiveness and attachment among employees and potential applicants. Referring again to the image of the construed external image (section 3.2.3), it can be followed that these studies indirectly argue for the link between CSR initiatives and OI. According to Greening/Turban companies must be attractive for potential employees in order to benefit from their knowledge and their skills. Also building on SIT they have shown that prospective applicants rather choose a company which obtains a positive image through its CSP, since values and norms are communicated which the

---

[231] The term 'disidentification' has been coined by Elsbach/Bhattacharya. They define disidentification as "[an individual's desire to (LR)] avoid negative distinctiveness by distancing themselves from incongruent values and negative stereotypes attributed to an organization" (Elsbach/Bhattacharya 2001: 393).

[232] See Carmeli et al. 2007: 985ff. Concerning the work outcomes see also section 3.3. Carmeli and colleagues also point out that their results provide further support for stakeholder theory (see 2.3.1), since managers need to consider a holistic approach of employees and other stakeholder groups, in addition to profit maximising concerns of shareholders and owners. See also 2.3.2.

[233] See Marin/Ruiz 2007: 254ff.

applicant incorporates into his self-concept.[234] In this respect CSR initiatives are interpreted in terms of enabling a competitive advantage. A study by Bhattacharya and colleagues suggests that the CSR initiatives can be used in order to "win the war for talent"[235]. They indicate that the CSR of a firm reveals its values and thus can be part of the "employee value proposition"[236], which in turn conducts into OI. Bhattacharya and colleagues also note the 'humanising' facets of CSR, since such initiatives portray companies as a contributor to society rather than as entity concentrated merely on maximising profits.[237]

Furthermore also *practice-oriented studies* carried out by well-known consultancies demonstrate that the CSR of a firm contributes to building strong bonds. Referred to a study released by IBM it is stated that CSR initiatives serve as an important argument for employees and prospective applicants to advocate on behalf of their firm.[238] Another study by The Boston Consulting Group employs CSR as part of bridging strategy and human resources. With regard to central future tasks that companies are confronted with in terms of human resources, managing CSR is considered as one of the key challenges, since it establishes deep going affiliation between the employees and the firm.[239]

4.4   Intermediate Result

The purpose of this chapter has been to bridge chapter 2 and 3 in order to answer the core question of the paper. Firstly, the underlying functional chain has been presented to explain the emergence of OI in the context of CSR initiatives (4.1). Secondly, each of the three processes that can be activated by a driver has been outlined in section 4.2. In particular, this has been affinity (4.2.1), which is when an individual identifies with an organisation whenever his values consistently match the values the organisation represents. Another process has been emulation (4.2.2), which takes place when the values of an organisation are gradually internalised by the employee. The last process that has been mentioned was categorisation and self-enhancement (4.2.3), which has been put forward by the description of seven mechanisms. Thirdly, section 4.3 served to recapitulate the theoretical reconstruction, the scientific review, and the practice-oriented studies in

---

[234] See Greening/Turban 2000: 256ff. "Individuals will report stronger job pursuit intentions toward firms described with positive versus negative CSP" (Ibid: 261). In addition to the placement of job, Greening/Turban also displayed that the probability of carrying out a job interview correlates with the CSP of a company. See Ibid: 271ff. For similar results see also the studies by Backhaus et al. 2002: 292-318; Siltaoja 2006: 91-111; Bhattacharya/Korschun 2006: 158-166.

[235] Bhattacharya et al. 2008: 37.

[236] Ibid.

[237] See Ibid. To highlight this aspect Bhattacharya and colleagues quote Berry/Parasuraman: "[...] a paycheck may keep a person on the job physically, but it alone will not keep a person on the job emotionally" (Berry/Parasuraman 1992: 24-34 as cited by Bhattacharya et al. 2008: 37).

[238] See IBM 2008a: 6. See also the closely related study IBM 2008b.

[239] See The Bosten Consulting Group 2008: 2ff.

order to provide insights to the question in how far CSR initiatives achieve OI. The following condensation can be advanced:

According to the three processes it can be summarised that each of these are in the position to be activated by CSR initiatives. As stated above it is not an either-or-situation implying that there is only one process that can be triggered off by the CSR of a company. Ideally, a CSR initiative triggers off all kinds of processes to let successfully identification occur. At this point it shall be noted again that for the achievement of OI, including the positive outcomes presented in section 3.3, a consistent information policy is required.[240] In terms of both the scientific review and the practice-oriented studies it can be inferred that they give relatively good reason to suppose that the CSR of a firm positively impacts the OI of employees. Hence, against the background of the three approaches discussed within the present section, CSR initiatives obtain huge potential to achieve identification of employees. Nevertheless these deliberations merely focus on the correlation of the two components of CSR initiatives and OI. Accordingly, other factors from which employees may build identification are not taken into account. Insofar we cannot deduce to regard CSR as being uniquely responsible to achieve OI. Thus, we can finally conclude a three-step saying that CSR initiatives of a firm (1) may trigger of processes which result into OI. Also, (2) they add up to a positive image perceived by employees, since the company is revealed as a humanised entity contributing to society. But (3) we cannot take it for granted that CSR initiatives are the only antecedent relevant for employees to augment identification.

5. Empirical Testing: CSR & Organisational Identification in Terms of a Telecommunications Company

Introduction

On top of the theoretical review an empirical testing in cooperation with a consultancy and a telecommunications company has been carried out in order to support the theoretical perspective with some empirical data. The notion to bridge theory and practice in terms of the present paper originates from the context of a practice seminar, which is held in the course of study "Philosophy & Economics" at the University of Bayreuth every semester since autumn 2008. Students of "Philosophy & Economics" work in different groups on future relevant topics, which are supposed to impact the potential of the telecommunications company. The seminar is supported by a consultancy.

---

[240] The notion to inform the employees about the companies' CSR initiatives becomes relevant in particular throughout the empirical survey in chapter 5. See also section 2.2.3 for the necessity to inform.

The telecommunications company

The communications company is a well-known multinational communications corporation.

The consultancy

The consultancy is a consultancy specialised in organisation development, change management and leadership.

The telecommunications company's CR

According to the corporate responsibility report the telecommunications company regards its corporate responsibility as "fundamental". In general the telecommunications company's CR strategy focuses on the engagement of various stakeholder groups and includes vital contributions to society and the environment.

Hypothesis

Building upon the theoretical review, the purpose of the empirical testing is to highlight the underlying question of the paper from another perspective in order to provide indication in how far CSR initiatives are able to achieve OI. For reasons of simplification model solely concentrates on two simple variables that already have been mentioned throughout the theoretical review: information (see sections 2.3.3 and 4.3) and identification (see 3.2.1).

Information

Among the voters a coherent theoretical understanding of what CSR is and in what way the telecommunications company is conducting certain CSR initiatives cannot be assumed. In addition, another objection might be that particular employees recognise many issues occurring in their working environment, but they are not aware that such activities fall under the CSR engagement of the telecommunications company.[241] Referring to section 2.3.3 companies must have in focus that their engagement has to be accurately communicated to their stakeholders. Given that CSR initiatives achieve OI, it is the logic precondition that the employee is acquainted with the CSR initiatives the telecommunications company is pursuing. Without knowing about the concrete activities, CSR cannot be linked to the two images of perceived organisational identity and the construed external image, which in turn implies that the CSR cannot be the driver for the achievement of identification. Insofar the first question will ask whether the telecommunications company employee is informed about the companies' CSR initiatives.

---

[241] This could for instance apply to the telecommunications company's Mobile Phone Data Collection, which is a mobile application that facilitates data collection in areas that are not connected to the internet. This system can be used by health workers in remote locations so that they are able to report potential disease outbreaks more rapidly. See Ibid: 34.

Identification

OI has been defined in this paper as a form of "social identification" and as "the perception of oneness with or belongingness to some human aggregate" (see 3.2.1).

Since theoretical background knowledge on OI cannot be assumed among the participants, the understanding of OI has been simplified to an easy-to-grasp-question. The understanding rather refers to categorisation processes based on Tajfel's definition of social identity.[242] Thus, the second question asks for the employees' identification in terms of being identified as a member of the telecommunications company's community.

Combining the two variables of information and identification, the following hypothesis can be formulated: The employees' identification with the the telecommunications company's community is related to the degree of being informed about the companies' CSR initiatives.

Design of the Survey

Rating System – Net Promoter Score

The questions the telecommunications company's employees were asked to vote for follow the concept of the so called net promoter score (NPS). The NPS is a management tool used by a consultancy that stems from the field of customer satisfaction research and has originally been used to gauge the loyalty of a company's customer relationships. It has been introduced by Frederick Reichheld in his Harvard Business Review article "The One Number You Need to Grow".[243] The NPS is regarded as a simplifying tool that reduces complexity and enables its users to analyse data fast and straightforward. A question is asked to a statistically valid target group which is to be rated on a rating scale from 0-10. Correspondent to the results the participants are categorised into three different groups: 9-10 voters, who are extremely satisfied, are labelled as 'promoters', 7-8 voters are passively satisfied ('passives'), and those who voted 0-6 are extremely unsatisfied known as 'detractors'. To get the NPS one has to subtract the percentage of detractors from the percentage of promoters. According to Reichheld's data research the average NPS is about 16%.[244]

---

[242] See section 3.1.2. "(…)[S]ocial identity will be understood a that part of an individual's self-concept which derives from his knowledge of his membership of a social group (or groups) together with the value and emotional significance to that membership" (Tajfel 1978: 63, emphasis in original).

[243] See Reichheld 2003: 46-54.

[244] See Ibid: 46 and 53. In terms of loyalty Reichheld notes that companies which garner world-class loyalty receive NPSs of 75% to more than 80%.

Platform, Target Group & Objections

With the help of the survey software on www.surveymonkey.com the survey has been set up online. A link to the survey was sent via email to a circle of the telecommunications company's employees whom the author got to know during his participation at a seminar. The email (see appendix I) was sent to 22 employees from one branch of the telecommunication's company including the request to forward the link to colleagues.

Particular background information concerning the target group has not been gathered. As far as the author knows, many participants of the survey have worked for the telecommunications company at least for two years or more. This information is not unimportant, since referring to section 4.2.2 one process of building identification can be achieved through emulation. Furthermore, the author received information from the consultancy that one branch of the telecommunications company resides at the moment in a phase of restructuring. That is, employees are confronted with changes among their working environment, which might imply different perceptions of evaluating CSR initiatives and the status of being identified with the the telecommunications companys' community.

Two Questions

As outlined above, the empirical testing has focused merely on the two variables *information* and *identification*. Accordingly, the survey consists of two questions that correspond to each variable. The questions have been formulated as follows:

1. "How well informed are you about the telecommunications company corporate social responsibility initiatives?",

   whereas 0 equates "I never heard anything of such initiatives", and 10 signifies "I am fully aware our CSR initiatives.

2. "Would you identify yourself as a member of the telecommunications company community?", whereas 0 equates "No, not at all", and 10 signifies "Yes, absolutely".

Results

The survey was open from February, 10th until March, 3rd 2009. Accordingly, the telecommunications company's employees were able to submit their votes within three weeks. In total 62 employees participated in the survey and rated the two questions.

In the following the results of the survey will be presented in a descriptive manner. To proceed in a structured way, firstly each question will be elaborated. Secondly, the results of the two questions will be presented in combination in order to spot the correlations between the variables. These are the results for the first question that aimed to detect in how far employees are informed concerning their company's CSR initiatives:

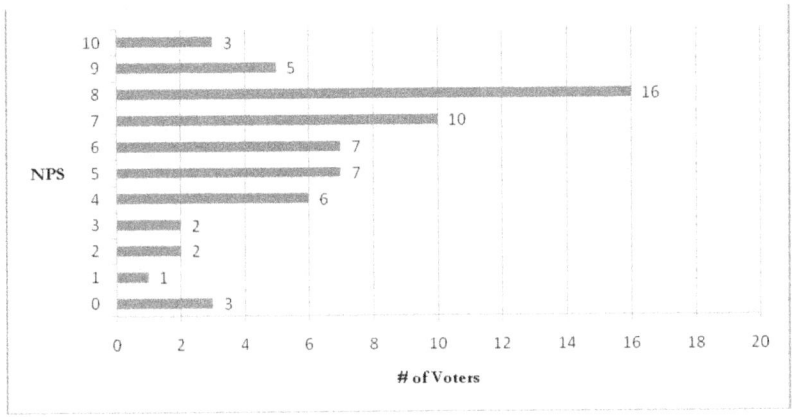

Figure 4: Bar Chart How Voters Responded To 'Information'.
Source: Author's diagram.

Based on the concept of the NPS the voters can be grouped into 12.90% promoters, 41.94% passives, and 45.16% detractors. Hence, the result of the NPS is -32.26%. The results correspondent to the second question, which was supposed to ask for the employees' identification with the telecommunications companies' community, are constituted as follows:

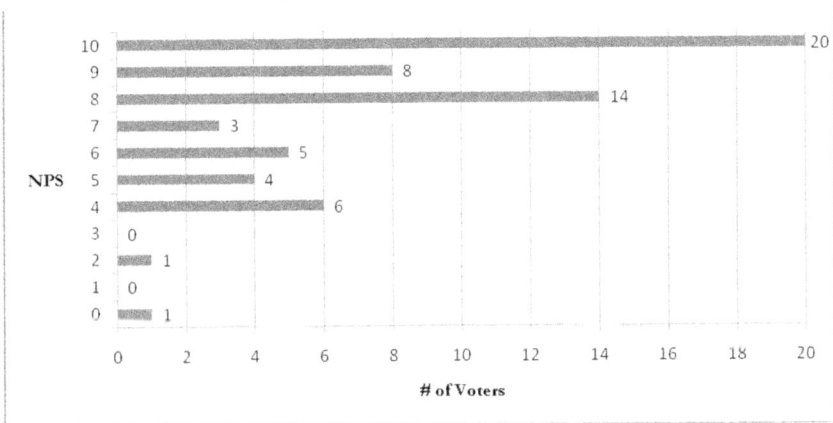

Figure 5: Bar Chart How Voters Responded To 'Identification'.
Source: Author's diagram.

In this case voters can be categorised into 45.16% promoters, 27.42% passives, and 27.42% detractors. The NPS is to that effect 17.74%.

Next, the results are illustrated, which reveal both votes each participant submitted. The sizes of the bubbles indicate the loading, meaning the bigger the bubble the more voters have chosen this specific combination. This is also visualised through the brightness of the bubbles.

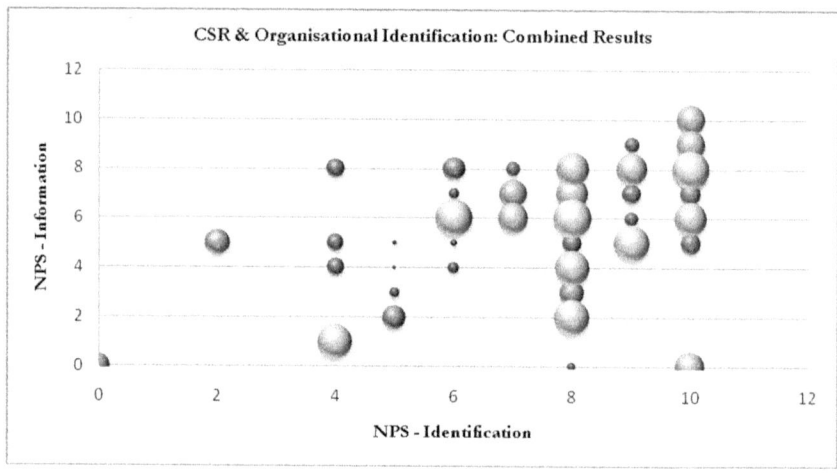

Figure 6: Bubble Chart Combining Both Variables.
Source: Author's diagram.

The specific combinations can also be categorised according to the three different groups that Reichheld proposed in his NPS concept. Each value (black) represents the number of voters correspondent to their combined votes. The subsequent table depicts each of the nine possibilities:

Identification / Information	Detractors 0-6	Passives 7-8	Promoters 9-10
Promoters 9-10	0	0	8
Passives 7-8	4	9	14
Detractors 0-6	13	7	7

Figure 7: Table of Combined Results.
Source: Author's diagram.

Discussion

Referring to the first question, the degree to what extent the telecommunications company's employees are informed about their employers' CSR initiatives, can be classified as poor, since only 8 out of 62 participants (12.90%) belong to the group of promoters and the results consequently reveal a negative NPS (-32.26%). Nonetheless one could interpret a positive tendency as 16 people (25.81%) rated their degree of being informed with an 8. Insofar a little more effort must be put into reporting about the telecommunications company's CSR initiatives needs to be done in order to improve towards a moderate level. Another aspect that is striking refers to the large group of detractors (45.16%). Hence, one could infer that either the information of the telecommunications company's CSR initiatives do net reach a wide range of employees, or a relatively large group simply seems to be not interested in how far the telecommunications company is performing CSR.

In terms of the second question the results differ from the first one. Almost half of all participants belong to the promoter group (45.16%), which indicates a relatively wide acceptance for the feeling of belongingness, to the telecommunications company's community. The positive NPS (17.74%) underlines this tendency. Thus, the degree of being identified with the telecommunications company among employees can be considered as moderate or even strong. Similarly as it has been the case with the first question, one could as well interpret a positive tendency for even more identification, as 14 out of 62 voters (22.58%) rated their status of being identified with an 8. Furthermore, the number of people, who do not identify with the telecommunications company at all, is vanishingly little, since only 2 participants out of 62 (3.2%) rated less than 4.

In comparison of the two questions it can be noted that the loading of the bars is in terms of being identified with the community relatively stronger compared to the degree of being informed.

So what can be deduced about the correlation between the CSR initiatives of the telecommunications company and the status of being identified with the telecommunications company community? Starting from the hypothesis that the identification of the employee with the telecommunications company's community is related to the degree of being informed about the companies' CSR initiatives, the following aspects can be put forward in correspondence to each cell based on figure 7:

Interestingly, those who belong to the promoter group of being fully aware of the telecommunications company's CSR initiatives are always absolutely identified with the the telecommunications company's community. This applies to 8 voters which is 12.90% (cell 3). Accordingly, none of the promoters in terms of information are merely identified with the telecommunications company's community on a poor or moderate basis (cell 1 and 2). Although the reason for that could be the CSR of the telecommunications company, it does not proof the hypothesis ultimately, because the causal connection could also be reverse. The employee is solely interested in the telecommunications company's CSR initiatives, because he feels such strong bonds to the community. In order to determine which aspect is the cause and which one is the effect, this issue deserves further investigation.

To achieve a higher degree of identification one could interpret cell 4 (6.45%) as value of potential. Cell 4 represents those respondents, who are not identified with the telecommunications company at all, but obtain a moderate degree of being informed about the telecommunications company's CSR. A rather negative explanation could be that the passive group perceived the CSR information so negatively with the effect of residing in the detractors group. Another view can be advanced insofar that although this group does not feel belongingness to the telecommunications company's community they perceived at least some CSR-information. As shown according to cell 1 indicating that a high level of being informed does not lead to disidentification, more information could result into a stronger feeling of being identified. This idea could also apply to those participants in cell 5 (14.51%) and cell 8 (11.29%), whereas in cell 8 the voters do not obtain any awareness of the telecommunications company's CSR.

Strikingly, the largest group that voted a combination one can find in cell 6 (22.58%). This cell stands for the telecommunications company's employees who are highly identified with the the telecommunications company's community but merely belong to the group of passives in terms of being informed about the telecommunications company's CSR. Such a relatively large group is a strong indicator for the fact that it is not only the CSR of the telecommunications company, which builds strong bonds with employees. Therefore, there must be other factors that are responsible for the attachment to the telecommunications company's community. This notion is also supported by the results of cell 9. Still 11.29% are a member of the identification promoter group without being informed about the telecommunications company's CSR initiatives at all.

Cell 7 covers the second largest group that selected a specific combination (20.96%). Those participants are completely uninformed concerning the telecommunications company's CSR and do not hold any feeling for being identified with the telecommunications company's community. In the first place one could argue in favour of the hypothesis as without the knowledge of the telecommunications company's CSR initiatives no identification can be the consequence. But again the problem of causality is present. We can only guess whether the employee is not informed because he is not identified with the telecommunications company or the other way round.

Conclusion

The results of the survey do not reveal definitive answers. Cell 3 in combination with cells 1 and 2 as well as cell 7 can be put forward in support of the hypothesis that the employees' identification with the telecommunications company's community is related to the degree of being informed about the companies' CSR initiatives. Nonetheless cell 3 and 7 have to be noted with reservation, since the results lack the problem of causality. On the contrary cells 6 and 9 indicate answers to the disadvantage of the hypothesis. At least they highlight that the image of being identified with the the telecommunications company's community also derives from other factors apart from the telecommunications company's CSR. Therefore, the following conclusion can be stated to some degree: CSR initiatives may have a positive effect on the employees' identification but they are not the only component that contributes to the feeling of being identified with the employer.

Accordingly, the present findings suggest a necessity of further research. In order to find out other reasons for the identification specified questions on why the telecommunications company's employees identify with the telecommunications company would be one field of investigation. Another aspect that deserves further research is in how far employees react to certain types of CSR initiatives. Against the background of the present thesis, CSR initiatives have been characterised according to a rather broadened understanding which subsumed different activities to a wide explanation of CSR initiatives. It would be of interest whether employees respond in terms of identification in a different manner as to e.g. corporate volunteering compared to corporate sponsoring. Consequently, a refined analysis is required in what way a certain CSR initiative evokes a specific effect related to the employees' identification.

In addition to this, another facet that deserves critique is the evaluation method of the NPS. The results presented above have been categorised according to specific thresholds according to the NPS concept. As already mentioned throughout the discussion, completely different results and conclusions would have been conducted, if only e.g. voters rating an 8 were counted as promoters.

Guidance

Starting from the overall objective to build stronger bonds with the telecommunications company, what can be done in terms of CSR in order to move the bubbles from figure 6 further to the right? From the author's point of view guidance shall be rather approached from the employees' attitude towards CSR. Insofar directions can be provided from two sides:

One aims at those employees who already regard CSR as beneficial and appreciate the telecommunications company's engagement. This group of employees simply need to be provided with further information on the telecommunications company's CSR initiatives, although a distinctive degree ought to be considered, since too much information could result into counterproductive effects. Such information is already and could be communicated through the annual report, regular newsletters or specific seminars dealing with the telecommunications company's CSR issues. Moreover, activities related to corporate volunteering[245] would involve the employee more directly and could be a mean to let employees experience the telecommunications company's understanding of CSR. This would also have the positive side effect that the employee could rep-

---

[245] See for further details on corporate volunteering section 2.2.2.

resent the company towards other stakeholders, such as customers or the local community.[246] In particular, such guidance could apply to employees who voted the combination represented in cells 3, 4, 5 and 6, although it cannot be said ultimately, whether the employees' awareness of the telecommunications company's CSR initiatives originates from their appreciation of CSR, simply from the fact because they are identified with the telecommunications company's or from some sort of disidentification, as they are fed up with the telecommunications company's current policies. Therefore, to put it in simple words, if employees like CSR, more information on the telecommunications company's CSR initiatives could be helpful for the achievement of identification with the community.

The second side refers to those employees who disregard CSR. Such employees shall be first convinced of CSR before they can build identification from that. In this case one could argue with the help of Maslow's hierarchy of needs. First basic physiological needs need to be satisfied until one seeks to meet the needs represented on higher levels.[247] Accordingly, only in case the employee is for the most part satisfied and does not have to fear big changes such as the loss of his job, he may see sense in carrying out CSR initiatives. Otherwise, CSR initiatives would rather obtain a counterproductive effect, since employees would wonder why their company spends budget on CSR, but not on their job. As a consequence the CSR ought to be in line with the current business process as well as what the firm is communicating though its organisational identity so that employees do not get irritated. Thus, to put it again in simple words, if employees dislike CSR, the telecommunications company should first try to acquire the employees' recognition of CSR, before CSR initiatives could be used as a driver to achieve identification. Such a strategy could apply to voters represented through cells 7, 8 and 9.

Outlook

Limitations and Future Research Perspectives

On top of the features that deserve further research pointed out in the conclusion another approach to more investigation could be carried out by opening the CSR-theme according to two aspects:

The *first* issue can be seen in other effects that result from CSR. Perhaps it is not only identification that can be built from the companies' CSR, maybe there are more positive employee relevant outcomes, which contribute to the firms' well-being such as problem solving capabilities, motiva-

---

[246] See section 2.3.2.
[247] See section 3.3.2 for Maslow's hierarchy of needs.

tion or creativity. The *second* issue is that CSR is not only relevant referred to employees as it also impacts other stakeholders such as shareholders, customers, suppliers and so forth. Most prominently large research has been conducted on the link between the CSP and the corporate financial performance.[248] According to literature other positive effects are observed in building an overall positive reputation to various stakeholders, more customer loyalty, and a more easy access to the capital market.[249]

Finally, one should note that unobserved variables can also influence the degree to which a the telecommunications company's employee feels identified with the telecommunications company's community. Also, it is conceivable that certain types of people may more strongly identify with the telecommunications company due to the CSR initiatives than others. For instance, highly competitive or achievement-oriented individuals may respond to other performances such as the market or financial performance stronger compared to activities attached to CSR. This issue deserves further investigation, too.[250]

6. Summary and Outlook

The present paper has pursued two main objectives: The *first* objective has been to review the correlation between CSR and OI from a theoretical perspective in order to provide answers to the core question of the paper: To which extent do CSR initiatives achieve OI?

Chapter 2 has dealt with the concept of CSR. After presenting the historical evolution of CSR elements of both CSR and CC have been taken in order to provide a broad understanding of the nature of CSR initiatives. Accordingly, it has been indicated that CSR is the more academic term describing the social responsibilities business has to society, whereas CC is the more managerial term enacting concrete actions serving community-relations. In this sense CSR initiatives have been defined as actions that foster a socially based purpose or a stakeholder group. With the help of basics of stakeholder theory and stakeholder management employees have been identified as 'first-class-stakeholder', since they obtain a peculiar role in many respects. Insofar companies have a deep interest in building strong relationships to their employees. In order to reach this concern, it has been suggested that CSR initiatives have the potential to achieve OI.

Therefore, chapter 3 has been subject to the concept of OI, which concentrated on what OI is and why it is useful for both companies and individuals. Drawing on the well-known SIA OI has been defined as "a specific form of social identification"[251] and as the "perception of oneness

---

[248] Many studies have investigated this link and have come to contradicting results. In favour of a positive correlation see studies by Alexander/Buchholz 1978; Cochran/Wood 1984; McGuire et al. 1988 and Waddock/Graves 1997. In contrast see for studies advancing a negative correlation Vance 1975 and Ingram/Frazier 1978.

[249] See for instance Promberger/Spiess 2006: 20ff.

[250] See Carmeli et al. 2007: 987f.

[251] Mael/Ashforth 1992: 105.

with or belongingness"[252] to an organisation. Besides the presentation of different dimensions and foci, two main images have been pointed out that strengthen OI: The perceived organisational identity is the members' assessment of the organisation's characteristics, where as the construed external image describes the member's belief what outsiders think of his organisation. Then, it has been argued that OI encompasses a huge significance for companies as well as for individuals. Companies benefit from OI of employees in many respects such as efficiency, or job satisfaction which in turn generates less turnover intentions. In terms of the individual OI satisfies various basic human needs.

Then, chapter 4 has served to bridge the previous chapters and to elaborate on the core question of the paper. To provide an understanding how OI emerges, a three-step functional chain has been put forward that has determined CSR initiatives as the driver to trigger off the three available processes of affinity, emulation, plus categorisation and self-enhancement, which in turn results into OI. It has been advanced that each of these processes are in the position to be activated by CSR initiatives. Moreover findings of various scientific studies as well as practice-oriented publications by well-known consultancies suggest similar results that the CSR of a firm positively impacts the relationship between the company and employees. In this respect a final conclusion has been shaped as follows: CSR initiatives of a firm may launch processes which conduct into OI and they also create an attractive image to which employees respond positively. Nonetheless it cannot be taken for granted that CSR initiatives are the only driver relevant for employees to build identification, since the processes for the emergence of OI, the scientific review, and the practice-oriented studies solely focus this very link between CSR and OI.

Such findings are supported to some degree by the empirical testing that has been carried out in cooperation with a consultancy and a telecommunications company. The *second* objective of the paper has been to provide additional insights to the theoretical review with the help of an empirical survey. For reasons of simplification the design of the survey has been reduced to merely two variables: information and identification. Building upon the underlying hypothesis that the employees' identification with the telecommunications company's community is related to the degree of being identified about the companies' CSR initiatives, the telecommunications company's employees have responded to two questions correspondent to the two variables. The results have not revealed definitive answers, since the votes can be argued in support of the hypothesis and also to its disadvantage. Nevertheless the results give suitable reason to speculate into the same direction, which has been outlined above according to the theoretical review. Insofar CSR initiatives may have positive effects on the employees' identification, but they are not the only component that contributes to the feeling of being identified with the employer.

---

[252] Ashforth/Mael 1989: 21.

Consequently, at this point the *limitations* of the present paper become unveiled. Against the background of a 'flat world'[253] including all the challenges companies are confronted with in the beginning of the 21rst century, the employees' identification is seen as one of the key factors for success. In view of the thesis the chances that CSR initiatives positively contribute to OI are relatively good. In spite of that the consideration of only one driver to result into OI does not meet the range of facets to be taken into account for the creation of identification. This aspect deserves further research. A similar notion applies to CSR, since the facets are more diverse than it has been assumed in terms of the broadened understanding in the present paper. Accordingly, it has to be detected which specific CSR initiative achieves a certain degree of identification. This feature deserves further investigation as well.

---

[253] "The World is Flat: A Brief History of the Twenty-First Century" is a title derived from the contemporary book by Thomas L. Friedman.

References

Abratt, R. (1989): A New Approach To the Corporate Image Management Process, in: Journal of Marketing Management, Vol. 5, No. 1, 63-76.

Ackerman, R./ Bauer, R. (1976): Corporate Social Responsiveness: The Modern Dilemma, Reston Publishing Company, Reston, VA.

Albert, S./ Ashforth, B. E./ Dutton, J. E. (2000): Organizational Identity and Identification: Charting New Waters and Building New Bridges, in: Academy of Management Review, Vol. 25, No. 1, 13-17.

Albert, S./ Whetten, D. A. (1985): Organizational Identity, in: Research in Organizational Behavior, Vol. 7, No.1, 263-295.

Alexander, G. J./ Buchholz, R. A. (1978): Corporate Social Performance and Stock Market Performance, in: Academy of Management Journal, Vol. 21, No. 3, 479-486.

Ansoff, H. I. (1979): The ABC of Strategic Management, European Institute for Advanced Studies in Management, Working Paper, 79-25.

Argote, L./ Insko, C. A./ Yovetich, N./ Romero, A. A. (1995): Group Learning Curves: The Effects of Turnover and Task Complexity on Group Performance, in: Journal of Applied Social Psychology, Vol. 25, No. 6, 512-529.

Aronson, E. (1992): The Social Animal, 6th ed., W. H. Freeman and Company, New York.

Ashforth, B. E./ Mael, F. (1989): Social Identity Theory and the Organization, in: Academy of Management Review, Vol. 14, 20-39.

Ashforth, B. E./ Saks, A. M. (1996): Socialization Tactics: Longitudinal Effects on Newcomer Adjustment, in: Academy of Management Review, Vol. 39, No. 1, 149-178.

Atkinson, A. A./ Waterhouse, J. H./ Wells, R. B. (1997): A Stakeholder Approach to Strategic Performance Measurement, in: Sloan Management Review, Vol. 38, No. 3, 25-37.

Backhaus, K./ Stone, B./ Heiner, K. (2002): Exploring the Relationship Between Corporate Social Performance and Employer Attractiveness, in: Business & Society, Vol. 41, No. 3, 292-318.

Barnard, C. I. (1938): The Functions of the Executive, Harvard University Press, Cambridge, Mass.

Beckmann, M. (2007): Corporate Social Responsibility und Corporate Citizenship: Eine empirische Bestandsaufnahme der aktuellen Diskussion über die gesellschaftliche Verantwortung von Unternehmen, Wirtschaftsethik-Studie No. 2007-1, Lehrstuhl für Wirtschaftsethik, Martin-Luther-Universität, Halle-Wittenberg.

Beckmann, M./ Pies, I. (2008): Ordo-Responsibility – Conceptual Reflections Towards a Semantic Innovation, in: Conill, J./ Luetge, C./ Schönwälder-Kuntze, T. (eds.): Corporate Citizenship, Contractarianism and Ethical Theory: On Philosophical Foundations of Business Ethics, Ashgate, Farnham and Burlington.

Berle, A. A./ Means, G. C. (1932): The Modern Corporation and Private Property, Macmillian, New York.

Berman, S. L./ Wicks, A. C./ Kotha, S./ Jones, T. M. (1999): Does Stakeholder Orientation Matter?: The Relationship Between Stakeholder Management Models and Firm Financial Performance, in: Academy of Management Journal, Vol. 42, No. 5, 488-506.

Berry, L. L./ Parasuraman, A. (1992): Services Marketing Starts From Within, in: Marketing Management, Winter, No. 1, 24-34.

Berthel, J./ Becker, F. G. (2003): Personal-Management: Grundzüge für Konzeptionen betrieblicher Personalarbeit, 7th edition, Schäffer-Poeschel, Stuttgart.

Bhattacharya, C. B./ Korschun, D. (2006): The Role of Corporate Social Responsibility in Strengthening Multiple Stakeholder Relationships: A Field Experiment, in: Journal of the Academy of Marketing Science, Vol. 34, No. 2, 158-166.

Bhattacharya, C. B./ Rao, H./ Glynn, M. A. (1995): Understanding the Bond of Identification: An Investigation of its Correlates Among Art Musuem Members, in: Journal of Marketing, Vol. 59, No. 4, 46-57.

Bhattacharya, C. B./ Sen, S./ Korschun, D. (2008): Using Corporate Social Responsibility To Win the War for Talent, in: MIT Sloan Management Review, Vol. 42, No.2, 37-44.

Blair, M. M. (2003): Shareholder Value, Corporate Governance, and Corporate Performance, in: Cornelius, P. K./ Kogut, B. (eds.): Corporate Governance and Capital Flows in A Global World, New York, Oxford, 53-82.

Bleicher, K. (1991): Das Konzept integriertes Management, Campus, Frankfurt and New York.

Böhm, S. (2008): Organisationale Identifikation als Voraussetzung für eine erfolgreiche Unternehmensentwicklung: Eine wissenschaftliche Analyse mit Ansatzpunkten für das Management, Gabler, Wiesbaden.

Bowen, H. R. (1953): Social Responsibilities of the Businessman, Harper & Row, New York.

Bowie, N. (1991): New Directions in Corporate Social Responsibility, in: Business Horizons, Vol. 34, No. 1, 56-65.

Breidenbach, S./ Matzak, B./ Stromer, C. (2008): Erfolgreiche Corporate Social Responsibility (CSR), Humboldt-Viadrina School of Governance, Studie 2008-1, Online-Publication: http://www.jk-kom.de/media/1/12167116187020/studie_erfolgreiche_ csr_2008.pdf.

Brink, A. (2000): Holistisches Shareholder-Value-Management: Eine regulative Idee für globales Management in ethischer Verantwortung, Rainer Hampp Verlag, München and Mering.

Brink, A. (2002): VBR – Value-Based-Responsibility, Teil 1: Theoretischer Ansatz zur Integration ethischer Aspekte in die wertorientierte Unternehmensführung, Rainer Hampp Verlag, München and Mering.

Brink, A. (2009): Spezifische Investitionen und deren Bedeutung für die Theorie der Firma, Unpublished Draft, Downloaded Online: http://www.pe.uni-bayreuth.de, 1-24.

Bruhn, M. (1998): Sponsoring: Systematische Planung und integrativer Einsatz, 3rd edition, Gabler, Wiesbaden.

Brundtland, G. (ed.) (1987): Our Common Future: The World Commission on Environment and Development, Oxford University Press, Oxford.

Bullis, C./ Bach, B. W. (1989): Are Mentor Relationships Helping Organzations?: An Exploration of Developing Mentee-Mentor-Organizational Identifications Using Turning Point Analysis, in: Communication Quarterly, Vol. 37, No. 3, 199-213.

Burke, L./ Logsdon, J. M. (1996): How Corporate Social Responsibility Pays Off, in: Long Range Planning, Vol. 29, No. 4, 495-502.

Carmeli, A./ Gilat, G./ Waldman, D. A. (2007): The Role of Perceived Organizational Performance in Organizational Identification, Adjustment and Job Performance, in: Journal of Management Studies, Vol. 44, No. 6, 972-992.

Carroll, A. B. (1979): A Three-Dimensional Conceptual Model of Corporate Performance, in: The Academy of Management Review, Vol. 4, No. 4, 497-505.

Carroll, A. B. (1991): The Pyramid of Corporate Social Responsibility: Toward the Moral Management of Organizational Stakeholders, in: Business Horizons, Elsevier, Vol. 34, No. 4, 39-48.

Carroll, A. B. (1998): The Four Faces of Corporate Citizenship, in: Business and Society Review, Vol. 100, No. 1, 1-7.

Carroll, A. B. (1999): Corporate Social Responsibility: Evolution of A Definitional Construct, in: Business Society, Vol. 38, No. 3, 268-295.

Carroll, A. B. (2000): Ethical Challenges for Business in the New Millennium: Corporate Social Responsibility and Models of Management Morality, in: Business Ethics Quarterly, Vol. 10, No. 1, 33-42.

Carroll, A. B./ Buchholtz, A. K. (2006): Business and Society: Ethics and Stakeholder Management, 6th edition, Thomson, Ohio.

Chatman, J. (1989): Improving Interactional Organizational Research: A Model of Person-Organization fit, in: Academy of Management Review, Vol. 14, No. 3, 333-349.

Cheney, G. (1983): The Rhetoric of Identification and the Study of Organizational Communication, in: Quarterly Journal of Speech, Vol. 69, No. 2, 143-158.

Clark, J. M. (1939): Social Control of Business, McGraw-Hill, New York.

Clarkson, M. B. E. (1995): A Stakeholder Framework for Analyzing and Evaluating Corporate Social Performance, in: Academy of Management Review, Vol. 20, No. 1, 92-117.

Cochran, P. L./ Wood, R. A. (1984): Corporate Social Responsibility and Financial Performance, in: Academy of Management Journal, Vol. 27, No. 1 , 42-56.

Cole, M. S./ Bruch, H. (2006): Organizational Identity Strength, Identification, and Commitment and their Relationships To Turnover Intention: Does Organizational Hierarchy Matter?, in: Journal of Organizational Behaviour, Vol. 27, No. 5, 585-605.

Collins, J./ Porras, J. (1991): Organizational Vision and Visionary Organizations, in: California Management Review, Vol. 34, No. 1, 30-52.

Crane, A./ Matten, D. (2007): Business Ethics: Managing Corporate Citizenship and Sustainability in the Age of Globalzation, 2nd edition, Oxford University Press, Oxford.

Cyert, R. M./ March, J. G. (1963): A Behavioral Theory of the Firm, Prentice Hall, Englewood Cliffs, New Jersey.

Davis, K. (1960): Can Business Afford To Ignore Social Responsibilities?, in: Calfornia Management Review, Vol. 2, No. 3, 70-76.

Davis, K. (1967): Understanding the Social Responsibility Puzzle: What Does the Businessman Owe To Society?, in: Business Horizon, Vol. 10, 45-50.

Deloitte (2007): M&A in Deutschland: Trends, Aktivitäten, Zielsetzungen, Strategien, Erfolgsfaktoren, Deloitte & Touche GmbH Wirtschaftsprüfungsgesellschaft, Online-Publication: http://www.deloitte.com/dtt/cda/doc/content/M%26A_in_ Deutschland_161107.pdf.

Dodd, E. (1932): For Whom are Corporate Managers Trustees?, in: Harvard Business Review, Vol. 45, No. 7, 1145-1163.

Donaldson, T. (1999): Making Stakeholder Theory Whole, in: Academy of Management Review, Vol. 24, No. 2, 237-241.

Donaldson, T./ Dunfee, T. W. (1999): Ties that Bind: A Social Contracts Approach To Business Ethics, Harvard Business School Press, Cambridge, Mass.

Donaldson, T./ Preston, L. E. (1995): The Stakeholder Theory of the Corporation: Concepts, Evidence, and Implications, in: Academy of Management Review, Vol. 20, No. 1, 65-91.

Dresewski, F. (2004): Corporate Citizenship: Ein Leitfaden für das soziale Engagement mittelständischer Unternehmen, Bundesinitiative „Unternehmen: Partner der Jugend", UPJ, Berlin.

Drucker, P. F. (2002): Knowledge Work, in: Executive Excellence, Vol. 19, 12-13.

Dukerich, J. M./ Golden, B. R./ Shortell, S. M. (2000): Beauty Is in the Eye of the Beholder: The Impact of Organizational Identification, Identity, and Image on the Cooperative Behaviors of Physicians, in: Administrative Science Quarterly, Vol. 47, No. 3, 507-533.

Dutton, J. E./ Dukerich, J. M. (1991): Keeping An Eye on the Mirror: Image and Identity in Organizational Adaptation, in: Academy of Management Journal, Vol. 34, No. 3, 517-554.

Dutton, J. E./ Dukerich, J. M./ Harquail, C. V. (1994): Organizational Images and Member Identification, in: Administrive Science Quarterly, Vol. 39, No. 2, 239-263.

Elkington, J. (2001): Enter the Triple Bottom Line, in: Henriques, A./ Richardson, J. (eds.): Triple Bottom Line – Does it All Add Up?, Earthscan, London, 1-16.

Ellemers, N./ De Gilder, D./ Haslam, S. A. (2004): Motivating Individuals and Groups at Work: A Social Identity Perspective on Leadership and Group Performance, in: Academy of Management Review, Vol. 29, No. 3, 459-478.

Ellemers, N./ De Gilder, D./ Van Den Heuvel, H. (1998): Career-Oriented Versus Team-Oriented Commitment and Bahavior at Work, in: Journal of Applied Psychology, Vol. 83, No. 5, 717-730.

Elsbach, K. D./ Bhattacharya, C. B. (2001): Defining Who You Are By What You Are Not: Organizational Disidentification and the National Rifle Association, in: Organization Science, Vol. 12, No. 4, 392-413.

Epitropaki, O./ Martin, R. (2005): The Moderating Role of Individual Differences in the Relation Between Transformational/Transactional Leadership Perceptions and Organizational Identification, in: Leadership Quarterly, Vol. 16, No. 4, 569-589.

Epstein, E. M. (1987): The Corporate Social Policy Process: Beyond Business Ethics, Corporate Social Responsibility and Corporate Social Responsiveness, in: Californai Management Review, Vol. 29, No. 3, 99-114.

Erez, M./ Earley, P. C. (1993): Culture, Self-Identity, and Work, Oxford University Press, New York.

European Commision (2001a): Green Paper: Promoting A European Framework for Corporate Social Responsibility, Online-Publication: http://eur-lex.europa.eu/LexUriServ /site/en/com/2001/com2001_0366en01.pdf.

European Commision (2001b): Mitteilung der Kommission betreffend die soziale Verantwortung der Unternehmen: Ein Unternehmensbeitrag zur nachhaltigen Entwicklung, Online-Publication: http://eur-lex.europa.eu/LexUriServ/LexUriServ.do?uri=COM:2002:0347: FIN:DE:PDF.

European Council (2000): Lisbon European Council: Presidency Conclusions, Online-Publication: http://www.consilium.europa.eu/ueDocs/cms_Data/docs/pressData/ en/ec/00100-r1.en0.htm.

Fombrun, C. J. (1997): Three Pillars of Corporate Citizenship: Ethics, Social Benefit, Profitability, in: Tichy, N. M./ McGill, A. R./ Clair, L. S. (eds.): Corporate Global Citizenship: Doing Business in the Public Eye, New Lexington Press, San Francisco, 27-42.

Foote, N. N. (1951): Identification As the Basis For A Theory of Motivation, in: American Sociological Review, Vol. 16, No. 1, 14-21.

Forstmann, S. (1994): Kulturelle Unterschiede bei grenzüberschreitenden Akquisitionen, Universitätsverlag Konstanz, Konstanz.

Foster, D./ Jonker, J. (2005): Stakeholder Relationships: The Dialogue of Engagement, in: Corporate Governance, Vol. 5, No. 5, 51-57.

Frankfurter Allgemeine Zeitung (FAZ) (2008): Einsatz nach Feierabend, in: Frankfurter Allgemeine Zeitung (FAZ), No. 133, 10.07.2008, B2.

Frederick, W. C. (1960): The Growing Concern Over Business Responsibility, in: California Management Review, Vol. 2, No. 4, 54-61.

Frederick, W. C. (1978): From CSR_1 to CSR_2: The Maturing of Business-and-Society Thought, Working Paper No. 279, Graduate School of Business, University of Pittsburgh.

Freeman, R. E. (1984): Strategic Management: A Stakeholder Approach, Pitman, Boston, Mass.

Freeman, R. E. (1994): The Politics of Stakeholder Theory: Some Future Direction, in: Business Ethics Quarterly, Vol. 4, No. 4, 409-421.

Freeman, R. E./ McVea, J. (2001): A Stakeholder Approach To Strategic Management, in: Hitt, M. A./ Freeman, R. E./ Harrison, J. S. (eds.): The Blackwell Handbook of Strategic Management, Oxford, 189-207.

Freeman, R. E./ Reed, D. L. (1983): Stockholders and Stakeholders: A New Perspective on Corporate Governance, in: California Management Review, Vol. 25, No. 3, 88-106.

Friedman, M. (1970): The Social Responsibility of Business Is To Increase its Profits, New York Times Magazine, September 13th, 1970, 32-33.

Friedman, T. L. (2005): The World Is Flat: A Brief History of the Twenty-First Century, Farrar, Straus and Giroux, New York.

Gallup (2005): Das Engagement am Arbeitsplatz in Deutschland sinkt weiter, Studie der Gallup GmbH Deutschland, Online-Source: http://www.presseportal.de/pm/9766/719311 /gallup_gmbh_deutschland.

Garriga, E./ Melé, D. (2004): Corporate Social Responsibility Theories: Mapping the Territory, in: Journal of Business Ethics, Vol. 53, No. 1-2, 51-71.

Gecas, V. (1982): The Self-Concept, in: Annual Review of Sociology, Vol. 8, 1-33.

Gioia, D. A. (1998): From Individual To Organizational Identity, in: Whetten, D. A./ Godfrey, P. C. (eds.): Identity in Organizations: Developing Theory Through Conversations, Sage, Thousand Oaks, 17-31.

Godfrey, P. C./ Hatch, N. W. (2007): Researching Corporate Social Responsibility: An Agenda for the 21st century, in: Journal of Business Research, Vol. 70, No. 1, 87-98.

Göbel, E. (2006): Unternehmensethik: Grundlagen und praktische Umsetzung, Lucius & Lucius, Stuttgart.

Goodpaster, K. E. (1991): Business Ethics and Stakeholder Analysis, in: Business Ethics Quarterly, Vol. 1, No. 1, 53-73.

Graves, S. P./ Waddock, S./ Kelly, M. (2001): How Do You Measure Corporate Citizenship?, in: Business Ethics, Vol. 15, No. 2, 17.

Greening, D. W./ Turban, D. B. (2000): Corporate Social Performance As A Competitive Advantage in Attracting A Quality Workforce, in: Business & Society, Vol. 39, No. 3, 254-280.

Greenwood, M. (2008): Classifying Employees As Stakeholders, Working Paper Series, Working Paper 4/08, Monash University, Department of Management, Online-Publication: http://www.buseco.monash.edu.au/mgt/research/working-papers/2008/wp4-08.pdf.

Habisch, A. (2003): Corporate Citizenship: Gesellschaftliches Engagement von Unternehmen in Deutschland, Springer, Berlin et al.

Hall, D. T./ Schneider, B./ Nygren, H. T. (1970): Personal Factors in Organizational Identification, in: Administrative Science Quarterly, Vol. 15, No. 2, 176-190.

Harrison, J. S./ John, C. H. S. (1996): Managing and Partnering with External Stakeholders, in: AME, Vol. 10, No. 2, 46-60.

Haslam, S. A. (2001): Psychology in Organisations: The Social Identity Approach, Sage, London.

Haslam, S. A. (2004): Psychology in Organisations: The Social Identity Approach, 2nd edition, Sage, London.

Haslam, S. A./ Postmes, T./ Ellemers, N. (2003): More Than a Metaphor: Organizational Identity Makes Organizational Life Possible, in: British Journal of Management, Vol. 14, No. 4, 357-369.

Hatch, M. J./ Schultz, M. (1997): Relations Between Organizational Culture, Identity and Image, in: European Journal of Marketing, Vol. 31, No. 5, 356-365.

Herzig, C. (2004): Corporate Volunteering in Germany: Survey and Empirical Evidence, Centre for Sustainability Management, Universität Lüneburg, Online-Publikation: http:// www. lu-phana.de/umanagement/csm/content/nama/downloads/download_publikationen/50-4downloadversion.pdf.

Hillman, A. J./ Keim, G. D. (2001): Shareholder Value, Stakeholder Management, and Social Issues: What's the Bottom Line?, in: Strategic Management Journal, Vol. 22, No. 2, 125-139.

Hogg, M. A./ Terry, D. J. (2000): Social Identity and Self-Categorisation Processes in Organizational Contexts, in: Academy of Management Reviews, Vol. 25, No. 1, 121-140.

Hogg, M. A./ Terry, D. J. (2001): Social Identity Processes in Organizational Contexts, Psychology Press, Philadelphia.

Hogg, M. A./ Terry, D. J./ White, K. M. (1995): A Tale of Two Theories: A Critical Comparison of Identity Theory with Social Identity Theory, in: Social Psychology Quarterly, Vol. 58, No. 4, 255-269.

House, R. J./ Rousseau, D. M./ Thomas-Hunt, M. (1995): The Meso Paradigm: A Framework for the Integration of Micro and Macro Organizational Behavior, in: Cummings, L. L./ Staw, B. (eds.): Research in Organizational Behavior, JAI Press, Greenwich, CT, Vol. 17, 71-114.

IBM (2008a): Corporate Social Responsibility: Integraler Bestandteil nachhaltiger Unternehmensführung und entscheidender Wettbewerbsfaktor, Online-Publication: http://www-935.ibm.com/services/de/gbs/pdf/2008/corporate-social-responsibility.pdf.

IBM (2008b): Attaining Sustainable Growth Through Corporate Social Responsibility, Online-Publication: http://www-935.ibm.com/services/de/gbs/pdf/2008/growth_through_csr.pdf.

Ingram, R. W./ Frazie, K. B. (1980): Environmental Performance and Corporate Disclosure, in: Journal of Accounting Research, Vol. 18, No. 2, 614-622.

Jackson, J. W. (2002): Intergroup Attitudes As A Function of Different Dimensions of Group Identification and Perceived Intergroup Conflict, in: Self and Identity, Vol. 1, No. 1, 11-33.

Jamali, D. (2008): A Stakeholder Approach To Corporate Social Responsibility: A Fresh Perspective into Theory and Practice, in: Journal of Business Ethics, Vol. 82, No. 1, 213-231.

Janisch, M. (1993): Das strategische Anspruchsgruppenmanagement: Vom Shareholder Value zum Stakeholder Value, Haupt, Bern et al.

Jones, T. (1995): Instrumental Stakeholder Theory: A Synthesis of Ethics and Economics, in: Academy of Management Review, Vol. 20, No. 2, 404-437.

Jones, T. M./ Wicks, A. C. (1999): Convergent Stakeholder Theory, in: Academy of Management Review, Vol. 24, No. 2, 206-221.

Kaler, J. (2002): Morality and Strategy in Stakeholder Identification, in: Journal of Business Ethics, Vol. 39, No. 1, 91-99.

Kelman, H. C. (1958): Compliance, Identification, and Internalization: Three Processes of Attitude Change, in: Journal of Conflict Resolution, Vol. 2, No. 1, 51-60.

Kreps, T. J. (1940): Measurement of the Social Performance of Business, in: An Investigation of Concentration of Economics Power for the Temporary National Economic Committee, Monograph No. 7, U.S. Government Printing Office, Washington, DC.

Loew, T./ Ankele, K./ Braun, S./ Clausen, J. (2004): Bedeutung der internationalen CSR-Diskussion für Nachhaltigkeit und die sich daraus ergebenden Anforderungen an Unternehmen mit Fokus Berichterstattung, Endbericht, Münster und Berlin, Online-Publication: http://www.ioew.de/home/downloaddateien/csr-end.pdf.

Lofland, J./ Stark, R. (1965): Becoming A World Saver: A Theory of Conversion To A Deviant Perspective, in: American Sociological Review, Vol. 30, 862-874.

Maaß, F./ Clemens, R. (2002): Corporate Citizenship: Das Unternehmen als "guter Bürger", in: Institut für Mittelstandsforschung Bonn (ed.), Schriften zur Mittelstandsforschung, No. 94 NF, Gabler, Wiesbaden.

Mael, F./ Ashforth, B. E. (1992): Alumni and Their Alma Mater: A Partial Test of the Reformulated Model of Organizational Identification, in: Journal of Organizational Behavior, Vol. 13, No. 2, 103-123.

Mael, F./ Ashforth, B. E. (1995): Loyal From Day One: Biodata, Organizational Identification, and Turnover Among Newcomers, in: Personnel Psychology, Vol. 48, No. 2, 309-333.

March, J. G./ Simon, H. A. (1958): Organizations, John Wiley & Sons, New York.

Marin, L./ Ruiz, S. (2007): "I Need You Too!": Corporate Identity Attractiveness for Consumers and the Role of Social Responsibility, in: Journal of Business Ethics, Vol. 71, No. 3, 245-260.

Maslow, A. H. (1943): A Theory of Human Motivation, in: Psychological Review, Vol. 50, No. 4, 370-396.

Matten, D./ Crane, A./ Chapple, W. (2003): Behind the Mask: Revealing the True Face of Corporate Citizenship, in: Journal of Business Ethics, Vol. 45, No. 1-2, 109-120.

McGuire, J. B./ Sundgren, A./ Schneeweis, T. (1988): Corporate Social Responsibility and Firm Financial Performance, in: Academy of Management Journal, Vol. 31, No. 4, 854-872.

McGuire, J. W. (1963): Business and Society, McGraw Hill, New York.

McWilliams, A./ Siegel, D. (2001): Corporate Social Responsibility: A Theory of the Firm Perspective, in: Academy of Management Review, Vol. 26, No. 1, 117-127.

Mead, G. (1934): Mind, Self and Society, Chicago University Press, Chicago.

Meyer, J. P./ Allen, N. J. (1997): Commitment in the Workplace, Sage, Thousand Oaks.

Mitchell, R. K./ Agle, B. R./ Wood, D. J. (1997): Toward A Theory of Stakeholder Identification and Salience: Defining the Principle of Who and What Really Counts, in: Academy of Mangement Review, Vol. 22, No. 4, 853-886.

Mowday, R. T./ Porter, L. W./ Steers, R. M. (1982): Employee-Organization Linkages: The Psychology of Commitment, Absenteeism, and Turnover, Academic Press, New York.

Mutz, G./ Korfmacher, S. (2003): Sozialwissenschaftliche Dimensionen von Corporate Citizenship in Deutschland, in: Backhaus-Maul, H./ Brühl, H. (eds.): Bürgergesellschaft und Wirtschaft – Zur neuen Rolle von Unternehmen, Deutsches Institut für Urbanistik, Berlin, 45-62.

Nair, S./ Pratt, M. G. (1997): Issues and Identity Conflicts in Multiple Identity Environments (MIE): The Case of Rural Physicians, in: Paper Presented at the Annual Meeting of the Academy of Management, Boston.

Neck, C./ Milliman, J. (1994): Thought Self-Leadership: Finding Spiritual Fulfilment in Organizational Life, in: Journal of Managerial Psychology, Vol. 9, No. 6, 9-16.

Organ, D. W. (1988): Organizational Citizenship Behavior, D. C. Heath and Co, Lexington, Mass.

Organ, D. W./ Podsakoff, P. M./ MacKenzie, S. B. (2006): Organizational Citizenship Bahavior: It's Nature, Antecedents, and Consequences, Sage, Thousand Oaks, London and New Delhi.

Patchen, M. (1970): Participation, Achievement and Involvement in the Job, Prentice Hall, Englewood Cliffs, New Jersey.

Porter, M. E./ Kramer, M. R. (2002): The Competitive Advantage of Corporate Philanthropy, in: Harvard Business Review, December 2002, 27-64.

Post, J. E./ Preston, L. E./ Sachs, S. (2002): Redefining the Corporation: Stakeholder Management and Organizational Wealth, Stanford University Press.

Pratt, M. G. (1998): To Be or Not To Be: Central Questions in Organizational Identification, in: Whetten, D. A./ Godfrey, P. C. (Hrsg.): Identity in Organizations: Building Theory through Conversations, Sage, Thousand Oaks, 171-207.

Promberger, K./ Spiess, H. (2006): Der Einfluss von Corporate Social (and Ecological) Responsibility auf den Unternehmenserfolg, Universität Innsbruck, Working Paper 26, Online-Publikation: http://www.verwaltungsmanagement.at/602/uploads/csr_working_ paper.pdf.

Reichheld, F. (2003): The One Number You Need To Grow, in: Havard Business Review, December 2003, 46-54.

Riketta, M. (2005): Organizational Identification: A Meta-Analysis, in: Journal of Vocational Behavior, Vol. 66, No. 2, 358-384.

Riketta, M./ Van Dick, R. (2005): Foci of Attachment in Organizations: A Meta-analytic Comparison of the Strength and Correlates of Workgroup Versus Organizational Identification and Commitment, in: Journal of Vocational Behavior, Vol. 67, 490-510.

Rometsch, M. (2008): Organisations- und Netzwerkidentität: Systemische Perspektiven, Gabler, Wiesbaden.

Schein, E. H. (1991): Organisationskultur: Ein neues unternehmenstheoretisches Konzept, in: Dülfer, E. (Ed.): Organisationskultur: Phänomen – Philosophie – Technologie, Schäffer-Poeschel, Stuttgart, 23-37.

Schöffmann, D. (2001): Corporate Volunteering: Gelebte Unternehmensverantwortung, in: Schöffmann (ed.): Wenn alle gewinnen: Bürgerliches Engagement von Unternehmen, Körber Stiftung, Hamburg, 11-22.

Schwalbach, J./ Schwerk, A. (2008): Corporate Governance und Corporate Citizenship, in: Habisch, A./ Neureiter, M./ Schmidpeter, R. (eds.): Handbuch Corporate Citizenship, Springer, Berlin and Heidelberg, 71-85.

Shamir, B./ House, R. J./ Arthur, M. B. (1993): The Motivational Effects of Charismatic Leadership, in: Organization Science, Vol. 4, No. 4, 577-594.

Shleifer, A./ Vishny, R. W. (1997): A Survey of Corporate Governance, in: Journal of Finance, Vol. 52, No. 2, 737-783.

Siltaoja, M. E. (2006): Value Priorities As Combining Core Factors Between CSR and Reputation: A Qualitative Study, in: Journal of Business Ethics, Vol. 68, No. 1, 91-111.

Sluss, D./ Ashforth, B. E. (2007): Relational Identity and Identification: Defining Ourselves through Work Relationships, in: Academy of Management Review, Vol. 32, No. 1, 9-32.

Smidts, A./ Pruyn, A. T. H./ Van Riel, C. B. M. (2001): The Impact of Employee Communication and Perceived External Prestige on Organizational Identification, Erasmus Research Institute of Management, Rotterdam, Online-Publikation: http://publishing.eur.nl /ir/repub/asset /10 /erimrs20000321133141.pdf.

Soppe, A. (2008): Sustainable Finance and the Stakeholder Equity Model, in: Cowton, C./ Haase, M. (eds.): Trends in Business and Economic Ethics, Springer, Berlin und Heidelberg, 199-228.

Strack, R./ Baier, J./ Fahlander, A. (2008): Talente fördern – Wissen bewahren, in: Harvard Businessmanager, March 2008, 24-36.

Swanson, D. L. (1995): Addressing a Theoretical Problem by Reorienting the Corporate Social Performance Model, in: Academy of Management Review, Vol. 20, No. 1, 43-64.

Swanson, D. L. (1999): Toward An Integrative Theory of Business and Society: A Research Strategy for Corporate Social Performance, in: Academy of Management Review, Vol. 24, No. 3, 506-521.

Tajfel, H. (1978): Social Categorization, Social Identity and Social Comparison, in: Tajfel, H. (Hrsg.): Differentiation Between Social Groups: Studies in the Social Psychology of Inter-Group Relations, Academic Press, 61-76.

Tajfel, H. (1981): Human Groups and Social Categories: Studies in Social Psychology, Cambridge University Press, Cambridge.

Tajfel, H. / Billig, M. G./ Bundy, R. P./ Flament, C. (1971): Social Categorization and Intergroup Behaviour, in: European Journal of Social Psychology, Vol. 1, No. 2, 149-178.

Tajfel, H./ Turner, J. C. (1979): An Integrative Theory of Social Conflict, in: Austin, W: G./ Worchel, S. (Eds.): The Social Psychology of Inter-Group Relations, Nelson-Hall, Chicago, 2nd ed., 33-47.

Tajfel, H./ Turner, J. C. (1986): The Social Identity Theory of Intergroup Behaviour, in: Worchel, S./ Austin W. G. (Eds.): Psychology of Intergroup Relations, Nelson-Hall, Chicago, 7-24.

Talaulicar, T. (2006): Unternehmenskodizes: Typen und Normierungsstrategien zur Implementierung einer Unternehmensethik, Gabler, Wiesbaden.

Tetrault Sirsly, C.-A./ Lamertz, K. (2008): When Does A Corporate Social Responsibility Initiative Provide a First-Mover-Advantage?, in: Business & Society, Vol. 47, No. 3, 343-369.

The Boston Consulting Group (2008): Creating People Advantage: How To Address HR Challenges Worldwide Through 2015, Online-Publication: http://www.bcg.com/impact _expertise/publications/files/Creating_People_Advantage_Summary_May_2008.pdf.

The Economist (2005): The Good Company, 20.01.2005, Online-Publication: http://www. economist.com/displayStory.cfm?story_ID=3555212.

Turner, J. C. (1975): Social Comparison and Social Identity: Some Prospects for Intergroup Behaviour, in: European Journal of Social Psychology, Vol. 5, No. 1, 5-34.

Turner, J. C. (1978): Social Comparison, Similarity and In-Group Favouritism, in: Tajfel, H. (Ed.): Differentiation Between Social Groups: Studies in the Social Psychology of Intergroup Relations, Academic Press, London, 235-250.

Turner, J. C. (1982): Towards A Cognitive Redefinition of the Social Group, in: Tajfel, H. (Ed.): Social Identity and Intergroup Relations, Cambridge University Press, Cambridge, 15-40.

Turner, J. C. (1985): Social Categorization and the Self-Concept: A Social Cognitive Theory of Group Behavior, in: Lawler, E. J. (Ed.): Advances in Group Processes, CT, JAI Press, London, Vol. 2, 77-122.

Turner, J. C./ Hogg, M. A./ Oakes, P. J./ Reicher, S. D./ Wetherell, M. S. (1987): Rediscovering the Social Group: A Self-Categorization Theory, Basil Blackwell, Cambridge.

Van Dick, R. (2004): Commitment und Identifikation mit Organisationen, Hogrefe, Göttingen.

Van Dick, R./ Christ, O./ Stellmacher, J./ Wagner, U./ Ahlswede, O./ Grubba, C./ Hauptmeier, M./ Höhfeld, C./ Moltzen, K./ Tissington, P. A. (2004a): Should I Stay or Should I Go?: Explaining Turnover Intentions with Organizational Identification and Job Satisfaction, in: British Journal of Management, Vol. 15, No. 4, 351-360.

Van Dick, R./ Grojean, M. W./ Christ, O./ Wieseke, J. (2006): Identity and the Extra Mile: Relationships Between Organizational Identification and Organizational Citizenship Behaviour, in: British Journal of Management, Vol. 17, No. 4, 283-301.

Van Dick, R./ Van Knippenberg, D./ Kerschreiter, R./ Hertel, G./ Wieseke, J. (2008): Interactive Effects of Work Group and Organizational Identification on Job Satisfaction and Extra-Role Bahavior, in: Journal of Vocational Behavior, Vol. 72, No. 3, 388-399.

Van Dick, R./ Wagner, U./ Stellmacher, J./ Christ, O. (2004b): The Utility of A Broader Conceptualization of Organizational Identification: Which Aspects Really Matter?, in: Journal of Occupational and Organizational Psychology, Vol. 77, No. 2, 171-191.

Van Dick, R./ Wagner, U./ Stellmacher, J./ Christ, O. (2005): Category Salience and Organizational Identification, in: Journal of Occupational and Organizational Psychology, Vol. 78, 273-285.

Van Maanen, J./ Schein, E. H. (1979): Toward A Theory of Organizational Socialization, in: Staw, M. B./ Cummings, L. L. (Hrsg.): Research in Organizational Behavior, Greenwich, Vol. 1, 209-264.

Van Dyne, L./ Ang, S. (1998): Organizational Citizenship Behavior of Contingent Workers in Singapore, in: Academy of Management Journal, Vol. 41, No. 6, 692-703.

Vance, S. C. (1975): Are Socially Responsible Firms Good Investment Risks?, in: Management Review, Vol. 64, No. 3, 18-24.

Von Clausewitz, C. (1832): Vom Kriege, in: Rowohlt Verlag, 15th edition, (1963).

Vos, J. F. J. (2003): Corporate Social Responsibility and the Identification of Stakeholders, in: Corporate Social Responsibility and Environmental Management, Vol. 10, No. 3, 141-152.

Waddock, S. A./ Bodwell, C./ Graves, S. B. (2002): Responsibility: The New Business Imperative, in: Academy of Management Executive, Vol. 16, No. 2, 132-148.

Waddock, S. A./ Graves, S. B. (1997): The Corporate Social Performance-Financial Performance Link, in: Strategic Management Journal, Vol. 18, No. 4, 303-319.

Walton, C. C. (1967): Corporate Social Responsibility, Wadsworth, Belmont, California.

Wartick, S. L./ Cochran, P. L. (1985): The Evolution of the Corporate Social Performance Model, in: Academy of Management Review, Vol. 10, No. 4, 758-769.

Welsch, H. P./ LaVan, H. (1981): Inter-Relationships Between Organizational Commitment and Job Characteristics, Job Satisfaction, Professional Behavior, and Organizational Climate, in: Human Relations, Vol. 34, No. 12, 1079-1089.

Wentges, P. (2002): Corporate Governance und Stakeholder-Ansatz: Implikationen für die betriebliche Finanzwirtschaft, Deutscher Universitäts-Verlag, Wiesbaden.

Westebbe, A./ Logan, D. (1995): Corporate Citizenship: Unternehmen im gesellschaftlichen Dialog, Gabler, Wiesbaden.

Wheeler, D./ Sillanpää, M. (1997): The Stakeholder Corporation: A Blueprint for Maximizing Stakeholder Value, Pitman Publishing, London.

Wienröder, H. (2006): Topfit für den Sprung nach oben, in: Handelszeitung, December 13th, 2006, No. 50, 21.

Wood, D. J. (1991): Corporate Social Performance Revisited, in: Academy of Management Review, Vol. 16, No. 4, 691-718.

Wood, D. J./ Logsdon, J. (2001): Perspectives on Corporate Citizenship, in: Andrioff, J./ McIntosh, M. (eds.): Perspectives on Corporate Citizenship, Greenleaf Publishing, Sheffield, 83-103.

World Economic Forum and IBLF (eds.) (2003): Responding To the Leadership Challenge: Findings of A CEO Survey on Global Corporate Citizenship, Geneva, Online-Publication: http://www.weforum.org/pdf/GCCI/Findings_of_CEO_survey_on_GCCI.pdf.

Sources from the Internet

http://circa.europa.eu

http://eur-lex.europa.eu

http://www.bcg.com

http://www.buseco.monash.edu

http://www.consilium.europa.eu

http://www.deloitte.de

http://www.economist.com

http://www.eur.nl

http://www.euractiv.com

http://www.harvardbusinessmanager.de

http://www.ibm.com

http://www.ioew.de

http://www.jk-kom.de

http://www.luphana.de

http://www.pe.uni-bayreuth.de

http://www.presseportal.de

http://www.sri.com

http://www.surveymonkey.com

http://www.verwaltungsmanagement.at

http://www.weforum.org

Date of last site views: 09.08.2010.